For those who lit the way
And those who will, going forward
For those we never should have left behind
For my guides and my guided

For the Carol Mitchell-Leons and Keilans
For the Professors and the Puffs
For all of the Antoines
And always,
For Azania

Greetings Reader,

My name is Asia Maxton, sometimes spelled as "Azya." At the time of this publication, I am a forty-two year old teacher, with a B.A and M.F.A. in theatre, a certificate in African-American theatre, and an expired teaching certificate, as of 2015. I am also a single mother to sixteen year-old Azania. This teaching memoir is a compilation of my experiences in Baltimore City Public Schools, from the time of my certification in 2010, to a few years after I resigned my position, and returned to contract teaching in 2015. You will find, within, anecdotes about my experience as both a full and part-time instructor, from 2010-2019. I will attempt to explain, here, why I let that last certificate expire, as many people have inquired over the years. The short answer is, I didn't want to be tempted to go back into the same system that led to the burnout I will detail within. Of course, most names have been changed in order to respect the privacy of my students and colleagues, but these stories are 100% true, to the best of my recollection.

I wrote the first draft of this book in one year, yet it has taken four years to get to this point of publication. It is hard enough to tell one's story, without having to re-read the most painful moments of our lives, three times over, to reach the threshold of successful editing. Even as I write these words, I am not certain that I have achieved this feat, but rest assured, you are receiving the best work I am currently capable of producing. The fear of judgment any non-fiction writer faces when telling their truth is one I have confronted, on multiple fronts, since beginning this process. The reason you are now reading these words is that I have finally convinced myself that the message is worth the risk.

Researching the following quote turned out to be quite the chore, as it has been attributed to, and adapted by, multiple sources including Ernest Hemingway, Paul Gallico, and Red Smith. I will conclude my introduction by directly quoting the latter here.

"Red Smith was asked if turning out a daily column wasn't quite a chore. 'Why no,' dead-panned Smith. 'You simply sit down at the typewriter, open your veins, and bleed.'"

BEFORE I BURN OUT

TALES, TRIALS AND TRIUMPHS OF A CITY SCHOOL TEACHER

AZYA MAXTON

RETHINK BOOKS, HARLEM 2020

ANTOINE

The fourteen year old seventh-grader with the chest tattoo and the gold grill, who told me, the second week of school that he was "grown" and I couldn't say anything to him, did some work in my class, for the first time, the week before Christmas break.

The second month of school, someone put an article in my box, something about butterflies, that relayed the story of a student who had almost slipped through the cracks, and the numerous opportunities his teachers had to try to reach him. After reading it, I asked the Physical Education teacher about Antoine, and told her the story made me think of him. She told me his biggest problem was that he never came to school. From that point on, whenever I saw Antoine, I told him how happy I was to see him at school, even when he refused to do work. One day, Antoine came to class, and didn't sit in the circle we always begin with. I asked him to join, and he declined. I told him, again, how happy I was to see him at school, and didn't resist his inclination to sit in the back. I went about my class instead, but when he continued to curse, even after a reminder about class expectations, I told him, calmly, that this act had earned him detention, then continued with the lesson.

He asked, later, for a pass to the nurse, and I inquired about the reason for his request. He told me he had "ingested some chemicals," and I wrote him a pass. The next week, when Antoine showed up for class, I told him, again, how good it was to see him at school, reminded him that he owed me detention, and when he refused to join our circle, reminded him, also, that, "in my class if you don't work, you don't play." He joined the circle. I smiled. We went over rules, rewards and consequences, as we always do. We did our breathe-in exercises for exercising the diaphragm and relaxation. As always, I promised to choose the most focused student to select our warm-up game.

When the student had selected the game, Antoine left the circle, going back to his familiar table in the back; but then, he asked me if I had a pen, and I told him he could get one at the table in the front of the room. When our warm-up game was finished, I asked the rest of my students to move to the front of the room, and to respond to the four questions I'd written on the board. After handing out pencils and paper, I circulated to the back of the room, and asked Antoine what he was working on. He pointed to the questions on the board. Before my other students had finished, earning their promised, and much anticipated, free-time, Antoine submitted his response. The first question, on the reflection assignment was, "What's the best part of drama class?" Antoine had written, "You learn to be true to yourself."

I told this story to a few friends, as justification for why I stay in such an intense and insane work environment. After serving his detention, Antoine continued to come to my class for lunch a few times. He told me about his car, and when I chastised him for driving without a license, he claimed that he'd let a friend drive it. Once he told me something about his weekend, and I asked a follow-up question, then paused, and said, "wait, do I want to know?"

When he insinuated that he was participating in illegal activities, I'd replied, "Well, you're probably not going to listen to me when I tell you to stop, but at least put some money away for a lawyer."

"Yeah, I got that too," he said.

After Antoine finally came to serve his detention, he began to frequently join the students who came to lunch in my room of their own volition. On one of these occasions, he actually cautioned another student, who was serving detention, that they should listen to me and do their work, so they didn't end up like him.

Another day, when he refused to work again, I asked him what he wanted to do with his life. He told me that he wanted to work on dirt bikes, the motorized kind that are illegal to ride in the city. He told me he had some experience in that area. I asked him if he knew it was illegal, and he said he did. "Okay," I sighed, "well, if you ever need anything, let me know."

A couple months later, Antoine was transferred out of the school. I was told he'd gone to a program that would help him make up for one of the years he had failed in school, so he could start high school the following year. I was also told, by a teacher who had run into his mother, that he was doing well.

To my dismay, a few weeks later, I saw Antoine on the news. He had attempted a robbery with an associate of his, and the victim had been shot in the arm. The story reported he was being charged with attempted murder, and as an adult. I wondered if the judge would know, or even care, that his father had been killed the year before. Rumor had it, that Antoine was much more in control of himself before that happened. Whatever the case, I was later informed that the charges were dropped down to "juvenile." I thought about the day I first met Antoine, when we had bumped heads and he'd told me, "I'm a grown ass man." He wasn't though. He was a misguided child, and I pray that one day he has a chance to be the man I caught a glimpse of those days in class, and even in detention.

DY'LONTE

He's always in detention in my room, not necessarily because I've given him this consequence, but because we have a break at the same time, and the vice-principal knows I don't mind. The week before Christmas, I had a revelation.

"You know what, Dy'Lonte? Your problem is, you're too fresh. Your hair is fresh. Your outfit's fresh (despite the fact that you're out of uniform). Dr. Phil says that 'Everyone has a currency,' and yours is being fresh. The problem, I see, is that your freshness doesn't match with your behavior. I bet…if I called your parents and told them to stop getting your hair cut, and to not give you your Christmas presents until your behavior changed, you'd be walking around here talking 'bout 'Yes Ma'am, No Ma'am, Yes Sir, No Sir.'"

He pleaded, "No, please don't."

I said, "You're only saying that because it will work. Who picks you up from school?'"

He went on to tell me how he lives with his dad, and his brother lives with his mom, because they don't have the same dad, but that his dad might pick him up from school.

I said, "Great, I can't wait to talk to your dad. I'll see you after school."

I did make it a point to try to meet him after school, but he told me it looked like no one was picking him up, and I should get his number from the vice-principal. I decided to ask his half-brother if he had the number, and he said he had it in his phone.

I dialed the number, and a man answered, stating that he was Dy'Lonte's dad. I told him the same story I'd told Dy'Lonte about him being fresh, and Dr. Phil's theory on currency. I even shared with him my personal story about my 7th grade daughter, and how she hadn't been able to wear the Jordans she received for Christmas 2016 until the spring, because she wanted to be fresh, in both senses of the word.

"That might work," Dad said, "I'll talk it over with his mother, and have her call you back."

"I really believe it will," I replied.

I stopped the student in question, before I left, because I knew they'd just received their report cards.

"How did you do?" I inquired.

"I did good," he replied.

Another student, interrupted, "He got C's and D's."

I called him over and explained "A is excellent, B is good, C is average, D is poor, F is failing. So, tell me again, how did you do?"

He said, "I did okay?"

I replied "With a lot of room for improvement?"

He responded, "Yeah."

As I was getting in my car, the other student added, "I feel you though. I wasn't allowed to get my hair cut for the last 3 weeks because of my grades."

I asked, "Did it help? How'd you do?"

He said, "I got A's and B's."

I never heard from Dy'Lonte's mom.

Fast forward to the New Year:

HIM: I'm so glad you didn't call my parents.

ME: I did call your parents...

HIM: I was so scared I wasn't gonna get what I needed for Christmas, but I had this little package...

ME: What did you need?

HIM: Fronts.

ME: As in gold teeth?!

I started to give up, again, in that moment, but I got over it.
Strangely enough, when I repeated this story to colleagues,
a few weeks after Dy'Lonte had left us, transferring to another
school, they told me that I was wrong. They relayed how he
and his brother used to come to school, looking poorly cared for,
sometimes unkempt, sometimes wearing the same clothes.
It seems they'd gone from one extreme to another.

THE CULTURE OF "SNITCHING"

One day, I had a conversation with my seventh-graders about when it's appropriate to "snitch." That discussion was inspired by another I'd had with two fifth, and two seventh-graders, one of whom had asked me, after admonishing one fifth-grader for snitching, "Miss Asia, don't you think that if I tell you something, you need to keep it to yourself?"

I replied, "It depends on what you're telling me. For example, if you told me that you were going to bring a gun to school, and shoot up the place, that's something that I would report. If you told me that you had a crush on one of these girls, I might keep that to myself."

I was dismayed to learn that almost half of them said they wouldn't "snitch" under any circumstance, and further dismayed when I used the school shooting example, that only about 30 percent said they'd tell no one but their friends.

So, I asked, "What about your teachers? What about me? I have a daughter your age."

One student, who has made great progress, since the beginning of the year, replied, "These teachers are trying to fail me, and make me repeat the seventh grade. If someone shot them, I wouldn't have to repeat."

I was so shaken by that statement, I had to end the conversation shortly after. It was a "get real" moment for me, like *I am dedicating my life to people who wouldn't even care if I was killed.* It was sobering, to say the least.

ON "BURN-OUT"

It's disconcerting to hear how many teachers are burned out. One week, I was making copies, and stopped to chat with a teacher I normally chat with. Another teacher I don't interact with much, was in the room as well, and the woman I was chatting with stopped to compliment him on his new haircut and shape-up. He thanked her, dryly, as if he was unimpressed with either his cut or the compliment.

I joked that the prior Friday he'd asked me how I was doing, and I'd replied "Tired." He'd said I looked tired, and I told him he wasn't supposed to say that.

"You know how people sometimes say 'I don't look like what I've been through?'" I laughed. "I guess I look like what I've been through."

After relaying this story to my female teacher friend, the male teacher admitted, "I don't think I can keep doing this. This is not what I thought education would be."

He went on to talk about his former (and now part-time) job, selling car parts, and how he never had to take work home. My other teacher friend replied, saying that she's been working on taking her life back, and now she doesn't work on Friday nights or Sunday. I told them both I understand. I took a 50 percent pay-cut to go part-time, and I still don't think I can handle another year.

I said, "They'll let you kill yourself, and they might send flowers to your funeral."

He said, "But you won't be able to smell them."

MORE THAN ONE BAD TEACHER

I found out that a whole class of 7th graders was failing math one week. Even my best student said she was failing that subject. When I asked her to explain she said they'd had a bad teacher one year. I told her it must have been more than one bad teacher, since I have seventh, and eighth-graders that can't even multiply. She said, "yes, two years of bad teachers."

So now, I was thinking about ways to integrate math with drama because that was not okay. Meanwhile, I hadn't seen my principal in nearly two months. Apparently, her long time love had been in the I.C.U. My vice principal was doing a commendable job of managing the school of over 400 students, despite that week's visit from the central office. You can always tell when "the suits" are in the hallway, and suddenly most of the classrooms have student work, and objectives posted in the hallway, with the exception of the teacher who was retiring that year. Her walls were bare. That amused me, but also made me sad, like the masks of tragicomedy that decorated my classroom door.

THEIR LIVES HAVE BEEN
HARDER THAN MINE
(I CAN LISTEN)

Naji and Yania came to my class most days at lunch. Taniyah usually joined them. Even on the days that I was scheduled to leave early, they often convinced me to stay. All of their lives had been harder than mine, and while I had finally acknowledged that my job made me insane, the realization that I was still saner than they were, made me indulge their requests. Earlier in the year, I was told that Taniyah lost her stepfather the year before. A few weeks later, she confessed that her biological father had been murdered a few years before that. I couldn't relate, but I could listen.

Naji told me about seeing her father abuse her mom. They're still in contact, and she cares for him. That week, she informed me that her father has six children. Three are by her mom. I had her older brother in one of my eighth grade classes, and her younger brother in my kindergarten. I liked them all a lot; even though I used to see Naji in the halls at the beginning of the school year, often angry, and defying my colleagues.

She went on to tell me, that Tuesday, how her dad had these other children, outside of his relationship with their mom. They were never married. (Shhh. My parents weren't either.)

But he tried to leave the mother of child number four, or maybe children four and five, for her mother. Eventually, her mom got tired, and now she tells her not to refer to "those" children as her siblings. But they ARE her siblings, she tells me, and it's not fair. Naji is right. It's not fair at all. This is why I stayed beyond my required, contracted hours because as they told me, "You're the only teacher we can talk to…Ms. J is always angry (understandably so), and Ms. S doesn't care." (Ms. S is probably just burned out.)

TEACHABLE MOMENTS

People kept telling me their stories, like they knew I was writing a book. I felt like I should travel with my laptop, or at least, a journal and a good pen. One of my favorite fourth-grade teachers told me one week that she was considering moving into an efficiency apartment so she could retire early. She said that most of her friends and family were telling her not to. I replied that I'd be the voice of reason, telling her to "go for it."

Fast forward to that Thursday night, I was watching my Shonda shows on t.v. T.G.I.T! I asked my 13 year-old wanna be trauma-surgeon daughter why she hadn't gone to bathe. She told me she still had to finish her homework. A few moments later, she relayed that she'd realized she didn't have the journal where she was supposed to record her reading response.

She said, "I can type the response, but I don't have my science homework."

Needless to say, I was disappointed, but trying to understand that she was becoming a young woman, I fell back. She spent the next hour, to hour and a half typing up her reading response, only to realize that the printer wasn't working. I asked if she could e-mail the assignment to her teacher, and she did. I tried to fix the printer to no avail, and sent her to bed, as I lay down myself, with six hours until we'd both need to rise.

16

In the morning, she tried the printer again, and with still no success, she began stomping around the house and slamming doors. My mother advised her to turn the computer off, and back on. This only exacerbated her frustration, as when she wasn't able to turn the computer back on, she couldn't even access her notes from the night before.

I suggested that she use my phone to access her assignment on the way to school, and take notes. My mom asked me if I could write a note to her teacher. I relayed that I could, but, since she had left her journal at school, and had an entire week to do the assignment, I was reluctant to do so.

On the way to school, my adolescent found that she couldn't pull up her Google Docs. She complained to me that she would receive a "U." I told her I couldn't imagine that she'd receive an unsatisfactory for just one missing homework grade. She told me it was two weeks worth of assignments. This made me a bit angry, realizing she'd had two weeks to complete her homework, but waited until the day before it was due. I told her that the lesson was more important than the grade, as I'd warned her several times about procrastinating until the last minute. She asked me to stop chastising her, and slammed the door one last time, upon our arrival at the school.

After the drop off, I decided to pull up an Audible book on my phone. The title was <u>The Book of Joy: Lasting Happiness in a Changing World</u>. The book was narrated by Douglas Carlton, but the main characters were the Dalai Lama and Desmond Tutu. My sister had offered me use of the app, and the book, a few days after I'd read the book <u>Desmond and the Very Mean Word</u>

by Archbishop Desmond Tutu with most of my students. I am a firm believer in synchronicity.

On this day, said book detailed the desire of parents to save our children from pain and failure, just as I was beginning to wonder if I'd been too hard on my child. It went on to examine the role of parenting in Holocaust victims and survivors, suggesting that children who have been spoiled by their parents, fared far worse in challenging circumstances, waiting on someone to rescue them; than those who had been brought up with survival skills, learning to cope on their own. I immediately turned off the recording and called my sister, to share the story of that morning.

I told her, "Moments like this give me faith, that if you're paying attention, signs will appear." I'd been wondering if, maybe, I was being too hard on my child. But this was as if someone had said, "You had a question, right? Here is your answer."

So, I decided that this was a story I should share with my students. I only had two classes on Friday, but I thought this was a lesson that had so many morals, it was worth including in my plan. After our usual agenda of reviewing rules, rewards, and consequences, breathing-in, and playing a warm-up game, I incorporated my story into my first class of sixth-graders, asking them to discern the lessons apparent in my story. We didn't get to the part of the lesson where they were supposed to high-light their parts in the next play they were reading, but I felt it was time well spent.

My next class of eighth-graders, however, was not as harmonious; there were a few unanticipated interruptions. Justin, a newer African-American student mentioned something about rich white kids, while Jordan, a white student, who had attended all year, interjected "There are rich black people, and white people who are poor, right, Miss Asia?"

Justin went on, "Yeah, but white people drag their parents."

Jordan countered, "My parents wouldn't let me get away with…"

I stopped to acknowledge that this was true, warning, "It is dangerous to group any category of people together. This is called stereotyping, and it leads to assumptions that are often not true, and makes things seem more simple than they are."

After wrapping up that conversation, I asked the students to move from the circle we begin class with, to the tables in the front of the room near the board where I provided instruction.

As we were moving, Jordan asked why the class wasn't receiving a free period, since the whole class wasn't there. I told him that the reason I didn't give them an entire free period was twofold:

1. The combination of eighth-graders I happened to have that morning was a culmination of those who had not signed up for an opportunity the rest were taking advantage of. I did not want to reward my remainders with an entire period of free-time.

2. I wanted them to know that while I am a firm believer in the philosophy of "Work Hard/Play Hard," I also intend for each

student who enters my room, on any given day, to leave just a little bit smarter than when they entered. I went on to explain that something they learn might be the difference between one concept on their high school interview, one question on their SAT, or one idea on their college essay.

So yeah, fast forward, to my students at the tables. Javon asked a question I can't remember the answer to, but I said, "my friend's brother is in prison for life because he was involved in a robbery where someone was murdered. At that point, they had a murder felony law, where if you were involved in a crime, and someone got killed, even if you didn't pull the trigger, you could go to jail for life."

One of my students looked at me, and said, "My father has life."

I'll never forget that look, or that moment. One of the other students, absentmindedly, said, "Who has life?" and the student repeated, "my father."

"I'm sorry," I said.

And he replied, "I don't care about that man."

His peers asked, "Have you ever gone to see him?"

He responded in the negative, and they said, "You should."

I asked, "Has he written to you?"

"Sometimes," he said.

"I agree with your friends," I offered. "He may have some things to teach you."

Speaking of teaching, no one taught me how to deal with these moments in my residency program.

JUSTIN

Because I had my seventh and eight-graders for seventy minutes, I worked with the P.E. teacher to allow them fifteen minutes of free time at the end of each period. My class was attached to the gym, so I usually sent a student to ask if we could join in for these last moments of play. Most days, the teacher agreed, and she acquiesced on this day as well.

As our students took over the courts and the adjoining stage, Justin came to talk to me. He told me that his brother had been in jail on a murder charge, but that the state had lost the evidence, which meant that his brother was coming home.

"I'm glad he's coming home," he said, "but between me and you, he killed that man." I didn't have the words to respond.

Justin came to lunch that day with my usual crew. Unprompted, he began to improvise a story about his life. He talked about the time when he would have a child, and picked up my water bottle, to improvise a baby.

"Justin, you wanna hit this blunt?" he imagined, using a dry erase marker as a prop.

"Nah, nigga, don't you see I got my baby?"

22

"I hate when people smoke around their kids," he interrupted, coming out of character, for a moment.

He went on to pretend that he was in jail. He spoke about friends putting money on his commissary, and shanking someone who had crossed him, then lying about murdering him, and laughing, later in his cell, at the lie he had told. His story ended with three-hundred plus friends attending his funeral.

I was simultaneously horrified, and entertained. His story was vivid. His mentality was horrific. I spent much of the thirty-minute period with my mouth agape and my eyes wide. The other students were amused at my amazement. When lunch was over, I just stared at my phone.

"Well, look at the time, I think you all need to get to class."

Justin protested, "I wasn't finished with my story."

I ended up, basically, pushing them all out of the door. I'd had enough for the week.

When I wrote about Justin on Facebook, a friend suggested that I share some Donald Goines or Iceberg Slim books with him, and encourage him to write his stories out. I thought this was a great idea, so I let him choose a Donald Goines book and ordered it for him online. Unfortunately, it didn't arrive until the last week of school, and Justin missed the last couple of days, so I never had the chance to share it with him. Maybe one day he'll read my words, and recognize his story here, and I can finally give him the book that is still on my shelf.

CREATE / DESTROY

Speaking of stories, when I told my friend the following story at dinner over our spring break, she couldn't stop laughing.

"That's the funniest story I ever heard," she said, but it's true, and it didn't start out being funny.

One reason a lot of teachers, self included, don't take many days off is that it often takes more work to prepare to be absent than it does to just show up. That year, I'd had three half days off, but only one with a substitute. Here's why.

In October, I decided to take a Monday off to attend my friend's wedding reception. I went in for my usual Friday half-day, then drove to the airport immediately after. I got into a small argument with a flight attendant on the way, that I swear to you was the result of accumulating stress. I was actually in the wrong (having tried to switch seats, when I didn't see anyone occupying a better one), but I already knew that (and was in the process of moving, when the occupant showed up), and didn't care to be chastised by the attendant.

Anyways, I had a wonderful time in Atlanta, reuniting with old friends, and I had booked my return flight for Monday afternoon, meaning I'd miss the two classes I generally taught on Mondays.

When I returned on Tuesday, there was a note from the substitute relaying that only a few of my seventh-graders had completed the assignment I'd left, and that many of them had actually left the room by the end of the period. I was not surprised by this revelation, but I was utterly dismayed to realize that many of my materials were missing. First, I saw that some of the puppets I had, most leant to me by the principal, were gone. Then, by the end of the day, I learned that the rubber stress ball we sometimes used for class warm-ups had disappeared; and I got word that someone had seen it torn up on the playground. There was also a kid's set of charade cards, part of a larger game, that had gone M.I.A. I was livid!

I made that class recreate the illustrated Charades cards, a set I use for my younger students, and I began planning a lesson that I hoped would teach them one.

The next week I asked the students to make models of a stage, using popsicle sticks and poster paper, and to label them with the stage directions they had learned. When the students who usually refused to participate declined to engage in the activity, I told them they could color a picture, or make models of anything else they chose. After about 30 minutes, I asked them to bring everything they had made or created to the back of the room where we always circled up for directions, breathing warm-ups, class games and reflection. Then, I instructed them to tear up anything they'd made that day and to throw it into the center of the circle.

Most were surprised, some were appalled, but I egged them on.

"That's right. Throw it in. Tear it up! Stomp on it!"

When their creations sat ruined in the middle of our group, I explained to them that that's what it had felt like to come back to missing and destroyed materials after my absence. I went on to explain that while it had taken them thirty minutes to create something, it took only thirty seconds to destroy.

"It's harder to create," I said, "it takes more time, more energy, more effort. Destruction is easy; and it's not just what you did to my materials, it's what I see you do to each other all day long. That (pointing to the newly created trash) is your self-esteem. From now on, in this class, we will build, and we will create; ourselves, stories, characters, and each other. What questions do you have?"

MYKWON

My daughter recently told me that she has changed her mind about being an OBGYN, and now wants to be a trauma surgeon. Her revelation led me to one of my own: that my family specializes in trauma. Thus, it should come as no surprise to me that the most traumatized students gravitate towards me, as a rule. Take for instance, just two weeks before spring break, a new student was sent to our school. I introduced myself in class, while calling him by name, as my students had already informed me that there was a new kid.

He did fine in class, but when I sent a student, per usual, to the gym to ask if we could join them for free time, I was told that the teacher would like to speak with me. I went to the gym, which was adjoined to my classroom, and another teacher was there with the usual P.E. teacher. She was the one who said, "We're fine with your class coming in, but how do you think MyKwon will do?"

I replied, "He did fine in my class, but I haven't read anything about him. What's up?"

She went on to tell me, "He's been kicked out of two schools for assaulting staff members."

I told her that I would keep an eye on him, and that I would also ask one of my students to keep a close watch.

Back at my classroom door, I pulled Carlos aside. Carlos was a student who had a lot of challenges at the beginning of the year, but who had become a leader in my class. I asked if he wouldn't mind staying close to MyKwon. I told him the truth about why I was asking, because he used to be just like that student, and because he had a brother in fifth grade who had anger management issues, so he was familiar with the signs most teachers also recognize before a behavior escalates. At the time, Carlos' little brother was being evaluated in a psychiatric hospital. He agreed to help, and promised to keep an eye on the student in question.

MyKwon did fine that day, but fast forward a week, and I found both he and Dy'Lonte in the hallway outside of my room. They told me that they were upset because they overheard someone in administration saying that they had drugs in their locker. They were adamant that this was a lie. I told them they needed a pass to come to my room, and Dy'Lonte agreed to get one. When I returned, five minutes later, the pair was sitting in the hallway outside of my door, again. They had not succeeded in obtaining a pass. I could tell they were still upset, so I said, "You can come in for five minutes and tell me what happened."

They told me their story, and I kind of believed them, but it was time for my first-graders to arrive. I told them they could stay if they each took a group to assist during the class. They agreed. Since the classroom had no interior walls, I knew I'd be able to keep an eye on everyone if things went awry, but I also knew that giving leadership roles to challenging students sometimes led to them living into the responsibility, as had been the case with Carlos.

Dy'Lonte did fine with his group, I took a group, and left the most self-sufficient groups to work on their own, reading the five-character play I had assigned them. When my group, and the self-sufficient groups had finished, I checked on MyKwon's. They were arguing about something, and asked me for assistance. When I asked if MyKwon had helped them, one student said he was no help. MyKwon asked another student, "Didn't I help you?" and when that student didn't quite agree, he got upset, and refused to stay with the group.

Fortunately, it was soon time for the first-graders to depart. After the teacher had come to collect her brood, I was left alone again with the two seventh-graders. Not a minute had passed before one of my colleagues entered my room, with his own key and said, "I just called school police. These two have been missing for two hours."

I apologized, acknowledging that I'd told the students they could stay for five minutes, but let them hang out for an hour. At the mention of school police, however, both students attempted to flee the room. I tried reasoning with them, "I'm not going to let anyone take you anywhere. I just told him where you've been. Calm down."

At some point, MyKwon bolted from the room, with my colleague, let's call him Mr. Freddie, following fast behind. Mr. Freddie called out, "When I get my hands on you... I am not the one. Code Purple. Lock down on the first floor."

Of course, where did the bolting student return? That's right. My room. Mr. Freddie came back eventually as well.

So now I had MyKwon, Dy'Lonte, and Mr. Freddie all standing around, tensely, in my room. After a few seconds of awkward silence, while everyone caught their breath and analyzed the situation, MyKwon said to Mr. Freddie, "You said 'When you get your hands on me...' When you get your hands on me what?"

To which Mr. Freddie replied, "When I get my hands on you, I'll take you to the office."

MyKwon was not buying this reasoning, and kept asking Mr. Freddie to "meet me in the middle." I presumed this meant the middle of my room, and that this was somehow an invitation to fight, and I was not with it.

Mr. Freddie must have interpreted MyKwon's words the same way, since he responded, "You have to come to me. Then it's self-defense."

MyKwon then grabbed a pair of scissors I had just set out for the art center in my kindergarten class. Really!?

Then he said, "I'm 'bout to catch a 187." For those of you who don't listen to rap music, this means a murder charge.

It appeared that MyKwon might be fronting for Dy'Lonte, so at this point I asked Dy'Lonte to leave the room. He refused, but then the Vice Principal entered, apparently on the phone with MyKwon's mom.

After quickly assessing the situation, he said, "Well, Mr. Freddie may be able to provide more details, but I am concerned about the scissors in MyKwon's hands." MyKwon proceeded to put the scissors down.

The vice principal, Mr. Manns, gave the phone to Mr. Freddie, and stepped into the hall. A few seconds later, Mr. Freddie asked me to hand the phone back to Mr. Manns, stating that MyKwon's mom had started cussing him out. All I'd heard from Mr. Freddie was, "No, I wasn't going to hurt him, but if he had come at me with those scissors, I would have had to defend myself."

I took the phone, with the intention of giving it back to Mr. Manns and heard MyKwon's mom saying, "Oh, you go hard huh? You think you're fucking..." Whoa! I stepped into the hall to search for Mr. Manns.

Meanwhile, in the short time Mr. Freddie was on the phone, both Dy'Lonte and MyKwon had left the building, then came back in. This time, instead of returning to my room, MyKwon was standing in the balcony of the school's foyer, shouting to the vice-principal, "I bet you're wondering how we got back in the building, huh?"

Mr. Manns was sitting on a bench on the other side of the foyer, near the front door, trying to calm Tyrese. Tyrese was Carlos' little brother, the fifth-grader who had just returned from a two-week psychiatric treatment. Tyrese was banging his head against the wall. Ignoring MyKwon, I started begging Tyrese to stop, for fear he'd hurt himself. I took over talking to him, as Mr. Manns began calling into the balcony, "Go back to class." Of course they didn't go back to class.

The vice principal had called both parents. MyKwon was saying, "My mom is coming, but she's going to spaz out." True to his word, when she finally came to pick him up, she cursed out Mr. Manns before she collected her son and sped off.

Just after that, Dy'Lonte's mom pulled up, but didn't get out of the car. Dy'Lonte said he was not coming out. She called him on his cell phone. He left the building, stopped to talk to his mom, then wandered off into the forest behind school grounds. Mr. Manns went to the car to talk to Dy'Lonte's mom, while I continued to sit with Tyrese, who had, finally, seemed to calm down.

Dy'Lonte came out of the forest, then walked past his mom's car, and in the opposite direction, towards the neighborhood streets. I asked Tyrese if he wanted to end up like MyKwon or Dy'Lonte. Tyrese, having witnessed the whole ordeal said, "of course not."

Mr. Manns returned, and relayed the story of how MyKwon's mom had cursed him out, to his surprise. She had, of course, not behaved that way when transferring him in. At one point, during the episode, Mr. Manns said to MyKwon, "your mother is a wonderful woman. I'm sure she'll be disappointed by your behavior." Mr. Freddie and I just glanced at each other, and chuckled, having heard her "choice words" over the phone. I asked Mr. Manns, "Why didn't Dy'Lonte's mom get out of the car?"

He said, flatly, "because she had the dog."

There was a brief pause before he admitted, "but she didn't get out because she didn't want to."

"Well, I think I've had enough of Baltimore City Public Schools for the day," I acknowledged, after realizing that my last class wasn't coming.

Mr. Manns looked at me, incredulous, "Really?" he said.

"Absolutely," I thought, but I just went to my room to pack up my things.

The next day I found a "504 behavior plan" in my mailbox for MyKwon. One of his accommodations included "remove sharp objects." I flashed back to another student I'd had in a fifth-grade class. After she'd attempted suicide, I was told I'd need to count each pair of my scissors after each class. The expectation that we be able to grant students easy access to materials while also managing these kinds of behaviors, without assistance, is another reason for potential burn-out in our educators.

My best guess is that MyKwon's behavior plan had followed him from his last school, but that due to the incident, someone realized I should have a copy too. As a contractor, who worked with the entire school, it was standard practice for me not to receive each student's behavior plan or I.E.P, but it was also against the law. The plan in my box was a C.Y.A. attempt.

THE MAN IN THE ARENA

"It is not the critic who counts; not the man who points out how the strong man stumbles, or where the doer of deeds could have done them better. The credit belongs to the man who is actually in the arena, whose face is marred by dust and sweat and blood; who strives valiantly; who errs, who comes short again and again, because there is no effort without error and shortcoming; but who does actually strive to do the deeds; who knows great enthusiasms, the great devotions; who spends himself in a worthy cause; who at the best knows in the end the triumph of high achievement, and who at the worst, if he fails, at least fails while daring greatly, so that his place shall never be with those cold and timid souls who neither know victory nor defeat."
- Theodore Roosevelt

My eighth-graders were instructed to choose between seven monologues and poems, one of which they would eventually be required to perform. The deal was they had to rotate between seven stations, and at the end of these rotations, they'd pick their favorite from the seven to work on for the next few weeks. As they rotated, I sat down with one of the groups, who happened to be reading *The Man in the Arena*.

After they'd read it, I asked them to explain what it was about. None of them were able to, but instead of re-reading, they kept trying to guess, mostly fumbling with useless clues, such as the internet source I'd pulled it from. The source was "The Obama Diaries," so one student guessed, "It's about Obama."

"Not quite," I responded, then asked them to read it again. I tried asking one student to read it aloud, and when they still couldn't explain it, kept them there, while allowing the other students to rotate through the various stations as planned. There was no apparent attempt, from any of the five students in the group to break it down, sentence by sentence, or question any words they might have had trouble with. They did not ask me, or each other, for help. They just flubbed. At one point, one of them said, "I feel like you're picking on us. Everyone else got to rotate."

After twenty-some minutes of what felt like pulling teeth, I instructed them to write their names on the piece. "I am choosing this for you," I said, "By the end of the term, you will be able to tell me what it's about." Then I asked the rest of the class to choose their favorite of the monologues and poems they'd rotated to, and bring it to the circle where we'd meet for closing questions and comments.

The following week, I sent students off to the stations that corresponded with the poem or monologue they'd chosen. I met with the students at each station, asking one volunteer to read aloud, then providing feedback that I asked each group to incorporate. I had started the class by providing a rubric, based on class input, listing five categories of a successful speech, and evaluating each category on a number system of 0-5. A rating of zero meant "no attempt," 1 was "you tried." 2 was "poor." 3 was "fair." 4 was "good." And 5 was "excellent."

I modeled a reading of one of my favorite poems from Marianne Williamson. I thought they might be familiar with it, since it had been in a couple popular movies, and at least one famous speech. The quote is often, wrongly, attributed to Nelson Mandela, but he did quote it at Bill Clinton's inauguration.

"Our deepest fear is not that we are inadequate. It is that we are powerful beyond all measure. It is our light, not our darkness that most frightens us. We ask ourselves, 'Who am I to be brilliant, beautiful/handsome, talented and fabulous?' Actually, who are you not to be? You are a child of God. Your playing small does not serve the world. There is nothing enlightened about shrinking so that others don't feel insecure around you. We were born to make manifest the Glory of God within us. It is not just in some, it is in everyone. And when we allow our own light to shine, we unconsciously give others permission to do the same. When we are liberated from our fear, our presence automatically liberates others."

I asked the students to rate me in each category using their fingers to indicate my score.

After I'd met with two groups, the students who had *The Man in the Arena* told me that they were "finished." I asked if this meant that they could recite it perfectly, and told them I would come to their station next. No sooner had I arrived at the station, than a few students entered class late, with a pass. I asked them to retrieve their poem or monologue and sit in at the appropriate station. One of the tardy students was the young man who'd told me I was picking on them the week before.

When I arrived at their table, I asked which student was going to recite the speech. No one volunteered, so I did my oft-repeated "Dishy-Dishy-Ice Cream." Of course, I landed on the student who'd said I was picking on him, and had come in late. As he struggled through the speech, I stopped to explain words and phrases I thought might be difficult to understand. When he'd finished, another student said to him, "I'd give you a one."

I told that student that the reciter didn't understand what he was saying, since he wasn't present when we'd reviewed the rubric. I handed out the rubric to the late students, and explained the system of evaluation. Realizing he'd just been rated poorly, the reciter lashed out at the evaluator. I stopped him, and asked him to attempt to explain again what the piece was about. He seemed stumped, but didn't try very hard either. I told the group that what bothered me about their class, and my school, in general, is that they didn't seem to even know *how* to learn. They didn't seem to grasp the concept that you have to be willing to make mistakes in order to learn. I gave the example of how in kindergarten we stumble through the alphabet, then in first grade we struggle to learn words, by second grade we're working to form words into sentences, by third — sentences into paragraphs, and by fourth grade, we're attempting to form paragraphs into essays; but if I'd used their method of learning, I'd still be reciting the alphabet in the fourth grade, because it would have been the only thing I'd mastered.

After breaking down *The Man in the Arena* again, sentence by sentence, I asked them to explain what the piece was about.

Finally, one student said, "It's about knowing how to fail. We don't get to be great without making mistakes."

"Yes!" I almost shouted. Now, to the reciter, I said, "Read the first line again. 'It is not the critic who counts.'"

"Who cares if he gave you a one?" I said, "You tried." No one expects you to be great on the first attempt, but you can't possibly be great without being willing to fail first."

That was one of those teachable moments that keeps me in this game, despite the fact that I may never win.

WHY I LEFT

After completing grad school in 2003, I almost immediately
went to a five-week arts exchange program in South Africa.
Shortly before traveling, however, I managed to get pregnant
by my African-American boyfriend. I didn't realize this reality
until I'd been in the motherland for two weeks. I took the money
I'd borrowed, with plans on moving to L.A. to pursue a career
in Hollywood, to fund my pregnancy, while unemployed. I was
sick for most of the nine months, so I didn't look for work
very hard, but I did go on at least one interview. I remember
meeting with someone about an editing position at Poetry.com.
I revealed to the interviewer that I was pregnant, and he said,
"that shouldn't keep anyone from hiring you." Nevertheless,
I didn't get the job.

I had moved back to Baltimore to be with my mom and went
back to work, part-time, a few months after delivering my child;
first, at a children's museum, then at another part-time job
teaching drama at an afterschool program in D.C, where my
sister happened to be principal. Not long after that, I found
more lucrative work as a traveling actress at a children's theatre
company. My mother had been laid off from City Schools,
as the director of alternative programs, a month before my
daughter's birth. I successfully predicted both that she would
be retained and then her final severance, prior to the city's fourth

round of cuts. After leaving the museum, and later the after school program, I found more supplemental hours, locally, as a substitute and tutor.

When my daughter was two, my mother went back to work. Now that my child could finally speak, I felt comfortable leaving her in a preschool program. I left the touring job and substituting after obtaining another part-time job as director of an after school program, and found more part-time work teaching drama through a local theatre's initiative. For the first five years of my daughter's young life, I managed to hold two to three part-time jobs steadily enough to provide for us both, with a great deal of support from my mom and sister, and, to my disappointment, little or none from her father.

I received childcare vouchers at our local YMCA, while still going into debt, for two of those years, and was ecstatic when a parent I'd met there offered to assist me in getting my daughter into a free pre-K program, that was not at the neighborhood school I'd refused to put her in, after observation. I volunteered at her school, the next year, in gratitude, before signing up for the Baltimore City Teaching Residency. I remember applying to the residency, just before the deadline, after journaling, and realizing it was what I wanted, or needed, to do. I was accepted into the residency in April of 2010, and began my training in June of that year. By August, I had accepted a position as a fifth-grade language arts and social studies teacher in Southeast Baltimore. This was only after being accepted, and later dismissed from, a charter school in my own Northeast neighborhood. Apparently, they thought someone was leaving, who later decided to stay. One of the directors of my program called this a win for me, stating that the school I was entering was the better school.

I had a grand mix of Latino, Greek, Black and White students that first year. The terms of the residency were that I'd be paid as a "step-four," first year teacher, while taking bi-weekly classes, and fulfilling assignments. On paper, I'd make $48,000 dollars a year, which was about a 25% increase from what I'd made working 2-3 part-time jobs. It was a lot of work! I managed to make it through the residency, but found that teaching was much less of what they'd taught us in my program, and much more about sustaining test scores on the standardized test. At that time, it was called the MSA, Maryland Standardized Assessment.

In preparation for this assessment, we took Baltimore City Benchmark tests quarterly. My school pretty much left me alone, until the end of the second quarter, when my Benchmark scores showed my students achieving at lower levels than expected. My principal's response was instructing me to begin using the provided curriculum books instead of the online curriculum provided by our district. As the MSA was fast approaching, she also offered coaching from a former teacher, who'd quit and become a sub, but who would assist me with instruction and test prep. It was suggested that this former teacher would model lessons for me, but the teacher refused, insisting that she'd rather co-teach. Ironically, she'd left her position because of the pressures of testing.

Additionally ironic was the fact that my special education teacher pointed out that our quarterly test, the Benchmark C, had a wrong answer on the key. I'd never thought to question the key, provided by the City before, despite the fact that we used these Benchmark Test scores as grades. Her pointing out this error led to me examining the rest of the test, and finding, then verifying with my colleagues, that there were, in fact, three errors on the key. This was the difference, for my students of a passing and a failing grade, a 60 and a 51, a 70 and a 61, an 80 and a 71, a 90 and an 81. I was appalled! I wrote to the city school's office of teaching and learning, about the error, after bringing it to the attention of my principal. I received no response from the city, or the system.

Meanwhile, my principal had relayed to our staff that the powers that be had insisted that she was giving too many effective ratings to teachers, and that from here on out, anyone who wanted an effective rating needed to "teach like your hair's on fire." Our system's Central Office had stated that we couldn't possibly have that many effective teachers, without an equal amount of effective test scores. My then-principal told me, at some point, that she really wanted to retire, but that she was holding out in order to get her son through an expensive private school. The irony of that statement was definitely not lost on me.

At the end of that year, budget cuts meant that my principal had to cut one member of the teaching team. My colleagues were up in arms, as no one wanted to leave our "good school," with the threat of transfer to one of the more challenging city schools. I stated in a meeting, of only teachers, that I was willing to leave. My reason was that my "good" school didn't seem to want to be great.

My principal cried, at the end of the year, as she shared that because I was the last hired, she'd need to let me go. I wasn't nearly as sad. I began interviewing, almost immediately.

I actually only went on one interview. My friend Ny'onna recommended me for a position at her school. They were hiring for a fourth-grade teacher, and she had just been made Teacher of the Year as part of the fourth-grade team, so I was coming highly recommended. I did well in my interview, I could feel it, but when they tried to end it, I asked, "Can I ask some questions?"

The interviewing team apologized for failing to ask this question before I did, and I asked what their expectations were for their students. One team member said, "We want them to be able to read, write, multiply and divide, but most of all, we want them to be good people."

She went on to tell me that they were starting a gifted program at that school, and that the best candidates to teach gifted children were gifted teachers. Wink-wink. The team also told me that they were very excited to hire someone who "thinks outside the box." I received, and accepted the position.

The following year was one of the most challenging of my teaching career. I realized, after accepting the position, that the school was incredibly "structured." My friend told me that she was going in early, that summer, to set up her classroom, and I responded that this was ridiculous, as they were bound to give us time during our professional development week to do so. She was right, and I was dead wrong. I had made the incorrect assumption that they'd just give us the time because it was obvious we would need it. After all, at my previous school, they had given us a couple of hours each day of the professional development week to set up. Here, we were allotted, only, a total of three to four hours during the week to set up our classrooms. This wasn't nearly enough time, particularly because as I moved into my class, I had to shake the desks of mouse droppings, and try to replace the broken teacher's desk with one that worked. At one point I was told that the teacher before me had decided not to have her own desk, due to limited space in the classroom.

Before the school year even started, I was in tears, as they explained at one professional development meeting, all of the forms that we would be responsible for completing regularly. There was a "data binder" we would need to create for these forms, and we started to receive numerous boxes of curriculum. As I would later joke, "They wanted us to fill out the forms that said that we checked the boxes that said that we filled out the forms."

How on Earth, I wondered, was I expected to "think outside the box" with so many literal boxes?

On the last day of Professional Development, before school was to start, I broke down, and started to cry, pondering how I could possibly live up to such ridiculous expectations, and still give my students what I knew they needed. With all of the rigidity in structure and curriculum, there was no room for the "out of the box" thinking the school claimed to have hired me for. How was I supposed to implement the project-based learning I'd spent the prior year studying in my special committee, or the arts-integration my previous jobs had prepared me for? How would I make space, in that tiny classroom, for those "teachable moments" that require require good teachers to go off script, when every moment needed to be accounted for, when so much data needed to be documented? I found it overwhelming and depressing. No sooner had my tears started to fall, then a literal earthquake shook the building, and we were evacuated. I will always remember the symbolism of that moment. Maryland almost never experiences earthquakes.

The school year was even tougher than I'd anticipated. I tried to stick to their boxes and forms, in order to maintain my position, and held after school tutoring in an attempt to give my students what I believed they really wanted and needed. On my grocery store trips every Sunday, I added cookies and apples to my list as incentives for students who stayed for coach class. I taught these classes voluntarily as to avoid any more potential rigidity in the school's paying after school program.

The woman who'd told me in the interview that they just wanted the students to be good people turned out to be one of my toughest challenges that year. One of Mrs. Tolson's two children would be among the seven I.E.P. (Individualized Education Plan) students I'd have in my class of 31. He was behaviorally challenged, and had severe A.D.H.D, and as a new teacher, with no assistant, I struggled to meet his needs. She moved him out of my class after I missed a few days in October due to a personal issue.

After my first classroom observation, she conveyed her disappointment with my teaching. I was conducting a math lesson, and remember her saying that she thought I'd have turned the class into a restaurant or something to illustrate the concept. I later joked that I didn't realize that general observations were supposed to be a show. If so, I would have sold tickets.

Her frustration with my lesson led to her inviting one of the veteran teachers, who taught my students in the 3rd grade, a year prior, to model a lesson for my fourth-graders, which, ultimately, just confused them about the concept of probability, which was evaluated differently in each grade. I felt Mrs. Tolson was very condescending in the conference that followed that modeled lesson.

She began by asking me, "So, what did she do first?" I answered that she'd modeled a problem.

"Good!" she exclaimed. "Then, what did she do?"

I answered, but I felt like she was treating me like a child. I was also upset because both she and the principal, who'd attended the model lesson, assisted the visiting teacher with disruptive behaviors during the session. They'd never done that for me. I continued to respond to her prompting for another twenty minutes, but was offended by the insinuation that I needed this basic instruction. I was, by no means, an expert at teaching math, and I was willing to learn, but this method of reflection felt phony.

I knew that she needed to be able to check the box which said she'd offered me assistance for my struggling class, many of which were three to four grade levels behind when they came to me. As Ny'onna once joked, "It's not like they gave you scholars, and YOU messed them up."

Still her support felt disingenuous, and it made me want to quit. I visited the office of the second vice-principal after the follow-up conference and shared my concerns. He relayed, quite honestly, that I came off as arrogant and unwilling to learn, to some of the staff, but that they didn't know, as he did, that I left school at the end of the day, but would come back at 4:00 and stay until they kicked me out of the building, around six or seven. He recognized my effort and dedication, and helped me to survive the year, by doing so. Shout out to him!

I recall my mid-year conference feeling more like an interrogation. Mrs. Tolson led the conference, and I was not prepared to defend myself against allegations that my data had not shown significant enough improvement. As far as I could tell, I was on par with my colleague who taught similar students, far above the lowest class, yet far below the "gifted and talented" class Ny'onna was leading. By my end of year conference, I was more prepared for what I might encounter, but I was still shaking. The principal noticed my visible anxiety, and inquired about the cause. I admitted that I'd been stricken by the mid-year conference, and was concerned that this final evaluation would prohibit me from the move I'd already decided to make. Fortunately, my final scores were high enough to enable my transfer. They were not, however, high enough to earn me a raise.

There was no air-conditioning in the tiny room I taught in that year, and one administrator would once ask another,

"Why does she take them outside so often?" It was the only incentive I knew to offer between subjects/lessons at the time, and my students were responsive. This was evident in that my class was most improved in math that year, according to the grade level contest the school sponsored. The teacher next-door to me, a Harvard Graduate, won most improved in Language Arts. Ny'onna's "gifted" class had won all of the awards for best scores. I bemoaned why any of us had been placed into competition in the first place. These kinds of contests were not conducive to my best teaching. This was one field where collaboration seemed a more beneficial strategy.

I remember, quite vividly, the note a student wrote to me that year where she stated, "You are putting too much pressure on us, and it's not working."

I also remember thinking, "I am doing to you all what they are doing to us, but you are absolutely right."

I walked out on my students three times that year, due to what I deemed extreme disrespect and the class and I would sometimes disagree, as to whether it was three or four times I'd left. I argued, "Regardless of whether it was three or four, if there are 180 days in a school year that makes 176 or 177 days that I stayed. Therefore, whether I went home three or four times, I stayed more often than I left." There's some math for you.

One of the times that I almost walked out, and was at my breaking point, my behavior specialist intervened. Once Mrs. Tolson removed her special-needs son from my class, I was left with thirty students, six of whom had documented learning

or emotional disabilities. Let's call the behavior specialist Mr. Brooks. Mr. Brooks walked in and said to my class, "How many of you know that you have something mentally, or chemically, wrong with you?" After a while, ten of my thirty students raised their hands. Mr. Brooks told them all to wait in the hall.
He went on to address the remaining twenty students. "The students in the hall know that they can not be expected to follow the same rules as the rest of you. Yet, you all want to match their behavior, instead of setting an example, and inspiring them to match yours."

Sharing this with a friend, recently, she was appalled by how very damaging that incident was to both groups. I will tell you, dear reader, that I have learned that dysfunction breeds dysfunction. In the same way that my twenty students were adapting to the behaviors of my more challenging students, many staff, self-included on several occasions, adapted to the sheer insanity of it all by behaving nonsensically ourselves.

For example, the day one student locked himself in the closet when I was on my way to lunch. I went to retrieve the key and unlocked the closet, then continued on my way without even checking in with the student. Of course, this was a student for whom these kinds of incidents had been commonplace. I do remember calling my father, during my break, and asking if I was becoming desensitized.

I didn't have any technology in my room, and when I asked the principal if I could possibly get more paper, given the fact that I couldn't project my work on to any kind of screen, she replied, "Miss Maxton, if I gave every teacher who wanted paper…"

as if to indicate that this was a ridiculous request, but I remember finishing her sentence, facetiously in my mind, like, "you might have a successful school."

One evening, in the beginning of the school year, I was staying at school late, per usual, when I happened to check my phone and saw that I had several missed calls. One was from my homegirl, Ny'onna, who left a voicemail saying that my vice-principal had an urgent message for me. I found the number, and called him. He told me that his urgent message was via the principal who wanted me to know that the bulletin board I'd just put up was unacceptable. According to my principal, and her superiors, the board I'd put up, for my current fourth-graders, which included their vision for an ideal classroom was not "grade-level work." I told my VP, that the assignment was one suggested by the school's proposed behavioral program, and that if it wasn't grade level work, this was because the students they'd given me were not yet on grade level. It was the beginning of the year. I couldn't possibly be blamed yet, for any learning deficits.

My idea to include this work on an initial bulletin board was actually spurred by one of the boxes of curriculum they'd given me. They were using a new behavior program called *Paths to Pax* which suggested students create a sort of vision board and statement that illustrated their ideas about their hopes for our class climate and culture. I thought it was a great idea to give them a voice in what our class culture should be. My vice-principal acknowledged that he believed in my intentions, but that our school would still not accept the bulletin board, with spelling and grammatical errors. His proposal was that I use pre-printed tests and quizzes on my bulletin boards to avoid such confusion in the future. I agreed to do so, but it was the first of many issues that would prove to be, not only antithetical to my teaching philosophy, but also antithetical to who I am as a human.

IDEALIST

Understanding that this "box-based" teaching was not allowing me to be great, I decided to search for a different school. Reading <u>The Law of Attraction</u> was instrumental in allowing me to create a different work environment, where I might have the freedom to instruct students in a way that would actually permit them to progress.

One day, on my way out of the local YMCA where I worked out, I ran into a former colleague, and told her I was seeking a transfer. She told me about a charter school that was affiliated with the high school she was managing now, that was arts-integrated and project-learning based. She said, "you would love them, and they would love you."

Soon after, I saw an open position at said school listed on a job site called Idealist. I sent my cover letter and resume, including a note with the words of my former colleague. Technically, I wasn't supposed to be able to transfer out of my current school, based on the requirements of my residency program, but they agreed to let me go if I could find work elsewhere.

When I arrived for my first interview, I was super clear that this was where I should be. I mean, they had a freaking stage outside the front of the school! The cafeteria was a café, and the classrooms were spacious and inviting, plus there were beautifully carved benches in the hallways to allow for alternate workspaces. A future colleague, who I'd invite to work with us later, once described her initial reaction to the school as "an educational heaven."

Noting the alternate work spaces forced me to recall a time when I'd tried to accommodate a special needs student whose I.E.P. stated that he needed "reduced distraction." I'd placed his desk in the hall, outside of my cramped classroom, before being told by the behavior specialist that this wasn't allowed. I understand the legalities, as I wasn't able to physically see this student in the hall, and thus, was unable to supervise him. This new school worked around this dilemma by having large windows in most classrooms where you could see the students in the hall. Later, I'd learn that the culture of the school allowed for trust between teachers, students and administration that allowed them to work in hallways even when we couldn't see them in every moment.

After three rounds of interviews, I landed the job. At the final interview, I ran into an acquaintance who had been managing after-school programming for the charter school. She said, "They need you."

I replied, "I need them."

She reiterated, "They need you."

She withdrew her program the year I was hired.

At my first interview I kept trying to show the hiring director, who was also the principal of the sister school my school was modeled after, my teaching portfolio. He kept saying, "Please sit down."

He went on to say, "We know who you are, and we believe you're capable. I just need to know if you have the time." I assured him I would make the time.

I started working at the charter school in the 2012-2013 school year. I was able to transfer my daughter there as well, only after being warned by the person who hired me, that bringing my child to the school I was teaching at might present a unique set of challenges. I'd already brought her with me to two former schools, so I thought I understood what he meant. However, the older my daughter got, the more these challenges increased.

For example, my first year at the school, my daughter's teacher decided to publish a book written by the class. In the biography section, my child had written, "She doesn't know who her dad is. She thinks he's a construction worker." I was incredibly embarrassed, as a teacher at the school, by this false assertion that I wasn't sure who my daughter's dad even was.

Nevertheless, in so many ways, working there was a wonderful experience. The school employed arts-integrated and project-based learning, both areas I'd developed some expertise in. In fact, I was on the "project-based learning" committee at my first assigned school.

I started teaching language arts and social studies to fifth and sixth-graders. The school was only in its seventh year, so these were the oldest children, and the plan was to gradually develop into a K-8 school, meaning my sixth-graders would be the first class to ever matriculate. The school was a replica of a successful sister school, so we often looked to them for guidance.

I truly enjoyed my experience there. I had the freedom to teach, without the excessive data binders and extensive lesson plans required by my previous program. Not only did the school allow me to spend the first few weeks on culture and climate, it was encouraged, and no one concerned themselves with grammar or spelling during that time. I taught argumentative writing and teamed up with the math and science teacher for an integrated lesson on food and gardening. I read <u>The Secret Garden</u> with my sixth-graders, and planted real fruit and flowers, with the assistance of a parent volunteer in the gardens that were already existent, but barren, in front of the school. My partner teacher read excerpts from the book and showed the movie, "The Omnivore's Dilemma." My unit was called "What Can a Garden Grow?" and his was "What Makes Food Good?" We collaborated to assign and grade a research paper about real food, based on their studies. I modeled each component of the paper in class.

We had a budget for supplies, and a budget for field trips. One of the field trips we went on that year was to a nursing home, where students shared personal narratives they'd written with their senior buddies, and were then invited to write stories inspired by the seniors for their storytelling unit, based on a local *Stoop Storytelling* series that was growing in Baltimore.

While doing research for the unit, I went to an audience-based *Stoop Storytelling* event. I'd planned on simply observing, for inspiration's sake, but after prodding from one of the hosts, entered my name as a potential story teller. Not only did I end up being randomly selected as one of the seven storytellers for this all audience based event, but I was the first to tell my story. The theme of the show was "Talents I didn't know I had." Ironically, I shared a teaching story about a former student who had been kicked out of an arts class, back when I was managing after-school programs. When I asked her to explain herself, I noted that her reasoning was poetic, and told her so. She shared with me that she did, in fact, write poetry, and ultimately, started a club at the school that I helped facilitate.

A parent arranged for my students to share their senior stories and personal narratives at the local children's museum; where she worked. She helped create a little fake stoop, and we brought them in to share their "senior stories" on a Saturday. Later, the mother who'd arranged for the museum sharing brought all of the students specialty lollipops as thank-you gifts for their participation. I loved collaborating with parents in this way. It felt like I was really educating as part of a community!

Of course, there were a few moments that weren't perfect. It was, as the hiring principal, had stated, a lot of work; and I cried one afternoon when I was chastised by the executive director for asking my students to help me with the administrative task of stuffing report cards. She didn't think it was a good idea for students to be handling paperwork with the grades of their peers, at all, despite the fact that they were folded. I thought she was probably right, but was annoyed that I was responsible for such tedious, administrative tasks. I just wanted to teach!

I did have a grade level assistant who was shared with my partner teacher. I'm not sure where she was that day, but we had grown very close. I remember her saying one day that she loved how I was consistently able to create "organized chaos" in my classroom. She was much more structured and practical than me, but I appreciated that, and she, in turn, admired my creativity.

The assistant, Yolanda, and I did bump heads a couple of times. First, when I was out for the day and she substituted for me, then went to my principal to complain that the "Henrietta Lacks" text I was working on with my sixth-graders was much too advanced. The principal agreed, and asked me to consider another text, telling me she'd taken the liberty of writing down a few options. I snapped on my leader that day, though I realized she was right in retrospect. I was just irritated that I'd told her my plans, and she'd not only not objected, but had seemed enthused. The truth is neither of us had bothered to read the text, in full, before I began the unit. I got over it, and lent my entire grant-given set of texts to a struggling first year teacher of high school, who was incredibly grateful, but quit the teaching residency I'd completed in the middle of her first year. Wise woman.

The second time I bumped heads with Yolanda was more minor. She was incredibly resistant to my request to put stickers on the spelling tests of students who'd done well, insisting that they didn't matter, in the grand scheme of education. I asked a student to explain to her their importance.

"Do you guys care about the stickers?"

The student's response was, "The stickers are *everything!*"

At the end of that second year, my assistant asked me if she would be working with me the following year. I told her I wasn't sure, but that I'd love for her to, and she told me that she definitely wanted to.

The last week of school, I happened to sit in on a planning meeting between my partner teacher, who was staying with the fifth-grade, and his new partner, the current fifth-grade language arts teacher. Sometimes I'd do things like this just because I wanted to learn. In the meeting, I heard the language arts teacher mention the role of my assistant, and I stopped to ask why she was including her in their plans.

"You didn't know?" she asked. "We get Yolanda."

I was livid. No one had bothered to mention this to me, particularly my principal, who was infamous for telling us teachers, "I don't like surprises."

I didn't like this surprise either, so I called my principal that evening, but despite her promise to return my call, she never did. I, in turn, took personal days during the two days of professional development Baltimore City had added to the end of our school year. I needed time to recover from what I considered to be a betrayal.

As karma would have it, I ran into Yolanda, sitting in the hallway, in front of the office, the week I returned to set up my new classroom for the following year. I'd been asked to move rooms, to my failed protests. After greeting her, my former assistant told me that she was there to resign. She'd spent the previous year lamenting the fact that her husband wasn't working, but was awaiting an assignment for a position with the secret service. He'd finally received a job offer, and told Yolanda that she could take some time off to pursue her degree. Well, well.

My principal, sensing my frustration, offered to allow me to sit in on the hiring process for a new assistant later that summer. On one phone interview, we spoke with a woman, Alicia, who was unable to meet in person because she had just been married in Georgia. She had been a full-time teacher in a challenging alternative school the year prior, and she wanted a reprieve. She relayed in the interview that she wanted to be "a master teacher," and it was obvious from her answers and demeanor that this was true. When we finished the interview I said, "If she wasn't married, I'd marry her."

My administrator told me that there were more interviews still to be conducted, and I told her, "People like that don't interview for long. Please hire her *now!*" She appeared dismissive, but she hired her soon after.

My second year, I received the opportunity to move up with the previous year's students, whom I'd already grown to know and love. This meant I would now be teaching outside of my elementary teaching certificate, and moving into middle school. We didn't have a set curriculum at my charter school, though we were encouraged to follow national teaching standards. At a local teacher's store, I found a project-based teaching guide on civilizations, a unit of study which was one of the requirements of the not so "voluntary" state curriculum for middle school. One of my proudest moments was the day I had thirteen different stations set up for students to rotate between, with the help of my new, extremely capable assistant. I remember my principal remarking, at one professional development meeting, on the fact that I was literally "skipping down the hall." I was that happy, because I was in my element.

One day I mentioned to my new assistant, Alicia, that our principal, Miss Loki, had traveled to New Orleans the year prior. Upon Miss Loki's return, she told me that she was "touched, moved and inspired" to have our students sojourn to New Orleans. At that point, I asked her if she'd been to Landmark, a life transformation course I'd attended, when pregnant with my daughter. The language she used indicated to me that this was the case. She told me that not only had she attended the program, but that our executive director, and my hiring principal had as well.

When I brought Miss Loki's suggestion up to my new, and highly capable assistant, Alicia asked, "Do you think we could make that happen this year?"

My immediate thought was "Ummm…no." But, in keeping with a lesson I'd learned from both my daughter, and my students, I decided not to share my doubts, and responded instead, "Sure." Alicia made it happen. With a lot of planning and passion, we were joined by her husband, a videographer friend, and three parent chaperones to take seventeen seventh-graders to New Orleans that spring for the first week of what would become an annual trip for our school.

Alicia made incredible plans for the trip, with very specific stops, and an extended stay in a New Orleans hostel, specifically designed for guests who wanted to be of service to the city. It was pretty surreal, and I still couldn't believe that she had made it happen. Not only had she ensured that our students could visit a swamp tour, a couple of museums — one where they would fulfill their service requirement — and a few local hot spots, but she had arranged the trip so that each chaperone could have a day or two to themselves to visit the city as an adult. The trip was so chock-full of activity that even I was worn out by our sixth day, in which our students climbed trees and ate beignets in one part of town, then rented kayaks and bikes in a nearby part of the city. Our students laughed about me falling out of a kayak on this trip. That night, which happened to be my birthday, we also had unlimited snacks and an open bar at the city's Rock 'N Bowl. Our students giggled again, when I ended up wearing bowling shoes outside at the end of the night because I'd forgotten to exchange my shoes. Despite all of the fun, we also managed to conduct nightly reflections regarding each day's activities. I was even able to work with individual students to complete some reading assessments on a few of the evenings, when we stayed at the hostel.

Fast forward to a few weeks after our return from that trip, when my second routine observation was planned. In accordance with our "What does it Mean to be Civilized?" unit, my students were staging a reading of the play, *Who Killed Marc Anthony?*, which was included in the project-based curriculum I had found at the teaching store. Some of my students were creating scenery and props, while one student directed a rehearsal of the play, the day my principal came to observe. I wasn't really concerned about what she saw that day, because I assumed she had a good overview of what we had been doing all year, and how this particular lesson related.

I'd started the year with the "Essential Question," *What does it mean to be Civil?* We'd attended a civil rights march with our sister school the first week of school. I tied this in with lessons about our class norms and school culture before moving onto this unit.

However, let us fast forward, again, to the day I met with my principal to discuss my observation and overall evaluation. She left me, for just a moment, with a document that detailed my observation, and included an overall score of 2.23.

After I'd had a moment to survey the document, she returned to the room, and asked where I'd like to begin. I asked, "2.23 out of what?"

She said it was out of a 4.0. I said, "Let's begin with the 2.23." She replied that I'd had some incidents with my colleagues that concerned her. I told her this had nothing to do with my class-room observation. Then she said that I was a drama teacher, and she wondered why my students hadn't memorized their lines. I reminded her that I was instructing an arts-integrated social studies class, and that the reader's theatre was there only to emphasize the importance of perspective in social studies. She had no further retribution, but I signed the evaluation, to my demise.

The next day, I regretted doing so, after calculating that a 2.23 out of 4.0 was a sixty-some percent, and I emailed my administrator, to tell her so.

She wrote me back, saying that she knew I was a wonderful teacher, and not to concern myself too much with the score.

I didn't concern myself too much with the score; well that is a lie, it haunted me; but I also knew that all I needed to receive my much-anticipated $6,000 raise was a "satisfactory" evaluation. I wasn't sure how this newly implemented score of "developing" would play out, but I was fairly certain that I would receive the 6 A.U.'s, or Achievement Units, necessary for my promotion. I will attempt to detail this system below, but, basically, what happened is that they went from a four category system to a five category system, at the end of the year, thus, allowing them to keep good teachers without ensuring us a raise.

I was so busy teaching my ass off that year (per usual), that I didn't even have time to question how that score would affect my raise until our Christmas break. Finally, I sent a message to Human Capital, wondering why the anticipated increase hadn't yet hit my paycheck. Someone wrote back to me, eventually, explaining that I'd actually scored just two points below satisfactory, due to an adjusted evaluation system, which meant I wouldn't be receiving my raise. I was outraged!

Allow me to explain. Baltimore City, realizing that more than 80 percent of teachers would be receiving a raise, due to proficient and highly effective scores, had decided to change the rules of the game — in May of the prior year! It's difficult for me, now, to explain the system they used to make the adjustment, but for those of you familiar with the general 0-100 grading system, let me put it like this. Whereas before an A would be 90 to100, an A would now be 94 to100: B, 84 to 93; C, 72 to 83; a D, 60-72 and a F, 59 and below. This allowed the school system to keep a whole lot of teachers who were rated, in the newly created category of "developing," without us receiving our raises, because while a previously average score of "satisfactory" would result in six achievement units (A.U.'s), a score of unsatisfactory would result in zero A.U.'s and the loss of your job. In this new system, an in-between score of developing would only yield three A.U.'s , or Achievement Units, allowing the system to keep many above average teachers, like myself (please read "really good" here) without needing to offer them additional pay.

The Union fought this agreement, as it should have, only to come to a settlement that gave most teachers a $1,000 one-time pay raise. However, ultimately, I lost out on $5,000 I had reasonably assumed would be mine, based on accurate calculations from the salary chart I was provided the year before.

Upon receiving this explanation from the office of Human Capital I wrote back, "Wow, and they actually got away with that?" There was no response.

I had a difficult time reconciling this revelation with my teaching. I guess I had always believed, despite being painfully aware of the history of this country, and world, that the adage was true: if I worked hard, and did what I loved, I would be rewarded accordingly. Now, realizing the fallacy of this belief, what exactly, I wondered, was I supposed to teach my students?

I heard a rumor that my principal had bragged to the principal of our neighboring high school that she hadn't awarded any of our teachers with a highly effective score. I also heard that his response was, "doesn't she want to keep them?"

I wondered if my executive director, someone I'd always deeply admired, knew that this was happening in our school. Did the education director, who had hired me, know as well? I was so disappointed at the mere thought.

At the beginning of the next year, I met with both the education director and my principal, as the former explained that the person they'd been working with at the school system had left their position. This meant the district was now stating that our school administration had missed the deadlines for observations. As a result of this miscommunication, they needed me to re-sign last year's evaluation with an earlier date. I looked at my formerly admired education director, despondent. Did he notice the low observation score, I was being asked to sign off on, once again? He seemed unfazed, and yet aware of my changed disposition. Despite my reservations, I signed the documents, but with a newfound promise to myself to leave my position at the first opportunity. I could no longer be a part of such shady dealings.

While this ended up being a good decision for me, I would advise any future teachers reading this, to consider advocating for themselves more, as opposed to quitting.

I went about my work that final year with three-quarters of the passion I'd demonstrated in my first two years at the charter school. At one point, my principal asked about my notable lackluster vibe, and I admitted to her that I was dismayed by the prior year's evaluation and outcome. I explained the effect it had on my income, despite her having advised me not to worry about it.

"That sucks," I remember her replying.

I'd also asked her, the year before, not to hire the current math specialist as a math instructor for the following year, citing text-based evidence that a strong team was essential for success in education. I knew, based on our history, that this teacher would be a poor fit.

My principal told me, "You've been heard...but you're good with those kinds of people." My final year, then, was spent, trying to compensate for this weak link, in our already challenging chain. While the rest of my team was stellar, it was already consuming work to help build a middle school that had not previously existed.

I found myself spent. Now, in addition to teaching social studies to three grades, and being asked to support language arts in two of those grades, conducting one "intensive" and an elective course in drama, plus supervising an advisory, I was also trying to supplement what I knew, and was told on repeated occasions, was weak instruction in math.

At the end of the year, the student, and parent, complaints began to pile up regarding the incompetent instructor, and my leader finally asked for my teammate's resignation. I had already submitted my own resignation, citing in it, "this profession is no longer sustainable."

On one occasion, my principal asked the two of us resigning teachers to speak to a group of students who had expressed concern about losing half of the teaching team. I thought, at the time, it was fair to ask this of me, since I'd voluntarily resigned, but not of the teacher whose hand had been forced.

I told my students, simply, "there may come a time in life where everything in you says run. When this happens, don't question it. *Just get out!*"

Before the year ended, my education director asked if I'd mind sharing some improvisation exercises at one of our professional development training sessions. I agreed, and we set up a meeting to discuss. He did ask me, then, why I was leaving.

"Is it the school or the system?" I believe, is how he framed it.

I replied, "Both."

"Well, we can talk about that later," he said, and we went on with our meeting.

At the close of the school year, my principal asked if I could write a post-dated resignation letter, so that they could begin interviews for my replacement. I had insisted on the post-date so that I could retain my health insurance for as long as possible.

WHERE TO NEXT?

People kept asking me where I was going next, and I told them that I wasn't sure. I'd believed in the power of manifestation for a long time, and I read an article on five-steps to manifestation, years ago, in a magazine, that I try to live by: the first step is knowing what you don't want; the second is knowing what you do want. I was only on step one.

I had about $4,000 in my savings account, and I knew that would be enough to pay my bills for the summer while I figured out my next move.

As summer began, I focused on a series of transitional tools I've learned to practice during seasons of change: read, write, pray/meditate, drink water, workout, create order. A few weeks into the break, my former colleague had a clothing swap at her house. Those invited could bring items they no longer loved to her home and search through the unwanted items of others for things they might use. Any unclaimed clothes would be donated to a local women's shelter.

As I sat on my friend's patio that evening drinking wine, I shared my transitional routine, adding that I was having the hardest time with the last step: creating order. I felt that my space resembled the chaos of my last couple of years and I just wasn't sure where to begin.

I was fairly depressed as I went to bed that night, unsure of my next move. I slept on the couch because my bed was broken, and although we'd attempted to fix it many times, a broken board in the frame caused me to sleep at an angle. I actually hadn't realized I was sleeping so chaotically until my sister stayed over one night, and I offered her my room. When she pointed out the problem, I realized it was only one piece in a series of dysfunction I had grown accustomed to.

At around 4 a.m. the morning after the clothing swap, I was awakened by smoke detectors. My mom came down the stairs, as I was sitting up, and told me that my room was on fire. She, my daughter and I made it out of the house with our phones, the cat and the dog before calling the fire department.

My room was mostly destroyed in the process, and I spent the rest of the summer using the insurance money to rebuild, and redesign it. It seemed the Universe had conspired to help me create that order I was having trouble with.

I'm reminded, as I write, of a conversation I had with my principal about an educational theorist I'd been intrigued by.

"What was it that he said?" I'd asked her. "Get rid of it, and start over?"

"Tear it all down," she replied.

Yes, I guess sometimes you have to.

SOCIAL-EMOTIONAL INTELLIGENCE

One of the highlights of my teaching career is that I was able to move up with two of my classes for three years. There are many takeaways from this opportunity, but one of my greatest was this: one of my classes (I began with them in 5th grade) was academically low, but possessed, collectively, a great deal of social-emotional intelligence. The second class (I started with in 6th grade) was academically advanced, in general, but did not possess the same degree of social-emotional intelligence.

At the end of my three years with these classes, the first class of incoming fifth-graders had much higher grades, cumulatively, than my more academically advanced class of incoming sixth-graders. The reason for this, to the best of my observation, is that the more socially advanced class embraced some of my big class goals, including: support each other, know your strengths and weaknesses, know when to ask for help, and use your resources. I had seven big goals for my class. In addition to the aforementioned four there was: develop a love of learning, think critically, and learn to read and write fluently.

Because my students, of lower "natural academic intelligence" learned to use their resources, support each other, know their strengths and weaknesses, and ask for help when needed, they did things like complete class assignments together (when doing so was not explicitly forbidden) remind each other of due dates, and even turn in each other's work. Meanwhile, my students who came in higher academically, would do things like fail to even turn in a take-home test on time, resulting in zeroes, that significantly impacted their grades.

At the time of this writing, these students are juniors and seniors in high school. I am eager to follow their journey, and see how these developments play out.

WHY I STAYED

It's the eighth-grader who's been to five middle schools who always hugs me in the hallway, the same one who asked to come to lunch last week with my usual seventh-grade crew, and stated, "this is extreme therapy," while listening to them vent about their lives as they usually do. It's me wondering who will listen when I leave.

It's the emotionally disturbed fifth-grader, who spent two weeks in a mental hospital, that I make sure to tell, "I love you," every chance I get. I guess I'm trying to make up for all the times he never heard it. It's the fact that this kid, who everyone's scared of, always says, "I love you too," even the day I refused to let him in my room because I didn't have the emotional bandwidth. It's all the students who are scared of him who know they're safe in my room, and who pull me aside to tell me when he's bullying, or lying about being a bully.

It's the seventh-grade brother of that same fifth-grader, who also leads my class, who, when complimented on his progress and leadership abilities, says in a deep baritone he reserves for instances of practicing maturity, "Thank you for your support. I appreciate it."

It's all the talks, and the fight I broke up the first week of school, that have led to this moment of maturity.

It's the other seventh-grade boy who made me cry twice this year by bursting through my broken door with the warning sign: "Broken Door. Please don't attempt to enter," and responding to my scolding with, "I'm sorry, Miss Asia. I love you." It's the time he led my class in a lesson on empathy.

It's the forty hugs I received at school the day I decided to count, especially the one from another behaviorally challenged fifth-grader who met me at my car, as I was leaving, and requested one.

It's all the hugs and "I'm proud of you's" they never received, that helped make them this way.

It's the moment of "Ohhh," my second favorite sound, that happens when a student finally understands something they've been struggling with.

It's the third-graders who always clean my room, who used to ask for something in return every time, but now correct each other with my words, "you should help because you want to, not because you're expecting something."

It's the joy of taking forty 1st and 2nd graders to their first play on a field trip.

It's the kindergartners who couldn't go outside one week because of their behavior, and had to read books that I told, "I'm sorry that you couldn't go out, but I hope you enjoyed the books," going back to their teacher and relaying, "So and so and so and so took off their shoes, and we couldn't go outside today, so we had to read books, but we enjoyed them." It's the parroting back of the language, as the other kindergartners left, with hugs, saying, "We enjoyed the books."

It's the pure innocence of my pre-k students playing with bubbles and sidewalk chalk.

It's all the times a student starts to lie, then responds to my side-eye with, "let me be honest," or my personal favorite this year, "Miss Asia, I can't lie to you."

It's the colleague who told me he's paid part-time but works full-time because of his "love for children." It's the fact that this brought me to tears. It's this same colleague who brought me the chart paper I requested, when the school's budget was exhausted, and threw in a box of pink sharpies just because.

It's the kids who ask their teacher, "If I'm good today, and finish my work, can I go help Miss Asia?"

It's the worst behaved students who make the best helpers.

It's the breakthroughs after the breakdowns. The laughter after the tears. The joy after the excruciating pain that accompanies this gig. It's knowing you're a soldier, and wondering if you'd fit in anywhere other than the battle ground. It's promising your family you'll get off the front lines, because it's maddening, then signing up for another tour of duty because well — you're already mad — and, yes, sanity is all so tempting, but the thought of it also kinda bores you.

THE GRASS IS NOT GREENER
ON THE OTHER SIDE,
IT'S JUST A DIFFERENT SHADE OF GREEN

People often ask me how long I've been teaching. The question is hard to answer. I usually tell them I've been working with kids since I was a kid. I started babysitting at ten. My first job was as an "executive consultant" at an organization called Black Community Solutions in Columbus, Ohio. I was really just a glorified mentor/sometimes tutor. I taught daycare in college, and also worked at a summer camp for ages 3-13. I taught college in grad school. After school, I worked at a children's museum, and as a touring actress for a few years, combined those jobs with an after school program, transitioned into substitute teaching and tutoring, managed after school programs, switched to teaching poetry and performance in the program I managed, while also teaching drama part-time. In those years, I was also a bartender at a local theater and at another arts venue, in order to earn extra cash and imbibe free art.

I spent five years teaching full-time: fifth-grade language arts and social studies at one school, then fourth-grade all subjects at another, and finally, moving up with my students for three years from 5th to 7th, and 6th to 8th grades, before resigning from the system. After dealing with the after-math of a house fire that summer, I returned to contract teaching later the next fall.

The impetus for my return is that I'd seen a viral video circulating on social media of a student being dragged across a room by a school police officer, due to insubordination. I saw a lot of teachers commenting on the videos, with statements like, "but you don't know what we deal with."

"Someone's got to bring the love," I said to myself, before responding to an ad for a contract agency that placed arts and technology teachers in schools. I started back with substituting with this agency for a couple of months, before they offered me a consistent part-time gig teaching drama. I thought teaching part-time might help salvage my sanity. Maybe it did. Maybe it didn't.

Sometimes people ask me if going part-time was any easier. I tell them it was six in one hand, half a dozen in the other. I used to be stressed out about too much work — bureaucracy and paperwork stress me out, particularly. Now, I was stressed because I didn't have enough money.

The year after my return to part-time teaching, I tried to switch back to college, but I couldn't make enough money starting as an adjunct to pay my bills, so I just switched contracting agencies. After two years with the agency, I asked to switch schools because there was an administrative change at my school that I wasn't comfortable with. The vice principal I'd grown to love was being reassigned, and the principal that hired me was being asked to retire. I'd noticed a "coup" from some of the teaching staff that wanted to be in administration, and I wanted no parts of it. I asked my agency for a different placement, but was told by the manager there, for whom there was mutual love and respect, that he couldn't place me in one of the better schools they had because there was already a team there who had bonded, and I would "stand out." I didn't think this was fair, but I did agree to interview with another school he suggested. When I Googled the school, I was troubled by the ratings and reviews. However, he convinced me to try to meet with the principal. The school leader wasn't there when I visited, but I met with another administrator. I asked as many questions as I could think of, to try to get to the root cause of the school's poor reviews. After many questions, it was revealed to me that the school did not have air-conditioning throughout the building, and that some of the class sizes were as large as thirty-five. I realized, as a new teacher, and a contractor, I would probably receive one of the rooms without air conditioning. As the school was solely for junior high students, that meant I would be trying to teach theatre to as many as thirty-five adolescents in one room, that might often be hot. I politely declined. Ironically, it was the chair of the theatre department at the college I wanted to work at that suggested that I try a different agency.

It turned out that the hiring director at the new agency was an acquaintance of mine, and that her partner was the former director of a summer camp my daughter had attended. When I first inquired, they had no openings, but she called me, just a few weeks before school was supposed to open for the year. One of their teachers had found another position, and there was one opening at a school just across the beltway from the one I'd left. She told me, honestly, that the school I'd be working at was "off the chain," and was one of their toughest. With time running out, I accepted the position, mostly because I liked the hours, 11:30 to 3:30 meant I could get to the gym and workout every morning after dropping my daughter at school, before I was too exhausted to do it. I thought maybe this would help me lose the 25 pounds of stress, and wine, weight I gained the prior year. Later, a colleague who used to work at the school I'd agreed to go to said she averaged about a bottle a day when she worked there. By the end of that year, I'd surpassed her average.

I worked out most days of the week, and moved a whole lot at work. Combined with the copious amounts of wine I consumed, miraculously I managed to maintain my weight, but I didn't lose any. I was praying that someday soon, my creative endeavors would pay off, and I wouldn't have to teach to pay the bills. I'd still work with youth, in some capacity — always — just not necessarily within this system.

My new school assignment was, literally, in the projects, in an area of town that's notorious for its *crazy*. Brooklyn, in South Baltimore, was beautiful, with waterfront views of the city's Inner Harbor, but it was also savage. As I drove over the bridge to work each day, I wondered if the rapidly gentrifying city would allow its poorest inhabitants to maintain this land. It just seemed like the property was too beautiful to avoid the grasps of gentrifiers. The only way I could imagine it is if the air or earth there was toxic, which would explain the behaviors I'd seen. I've since learned that there is a giant incinerator in this neighborhood.

We averaged one fight a week during my first month at the school, including the time one of my students threw a chair at another. The first fight was week one, on the playground. It wasn't my students, but I witnessed it. The second was two girls in the hallway, after my class, pulling each other's hair. I broke that one up. The third was the girl who threw the chair at one of my special education students who was bothering her. I had to write that one up, but in all honesty, I understood her frustration. The last fight was when KamRon, one of my more challenging students, tried to take a phone from a student who refused to relinquish his to me, after violating our "no phone during instruction" class policy. He was trying to ensure that the class received their free time that day. Another student broke that one up.

During one particular professional development training, we were asked to select a moment that solidified our decision to teach. Mind you, teaching is in my blood. My maternal grandmother was a teacher, my mom was a teacher (who went into management, and retired from administration), my sister taught for three years, and spent another year as a principal, two of my aunts are teachers, and I have been working with young people since my youth. However, one series of moments in my life does stand out as an impetus to commit to the profession. When my daughter was very young, I used to take her to the newly built playground near our house. Oftentimes, on those visits, I'd see some of the older kids cursing and carrying on, and I'd pull them to the side and say something like, "You see all of these little kids playing? They're looking up to you. They're going to want to be just like you when they grow up. Is your language and behavior something you want them to imitate?"

On several occasions, when I'd give this little speech, the recipient of my reprimand would begin to follow me around the playground. I started to understand that these youth wanted attention and structure so desperately, that they'd accept it even from the stern mama on the playground, who was just trying to ensure that her baby had a positive place to play. I believe this realization accounts for my dedication to teaching today.

KAMRON

KamRon and I got off to a rough start, but we'd been making progress. He didn't show up to my seventh-grade class until the third week of school, so he missed my whole *rules, routines and procedures* spiel. The first day, when he acted up, I tried being hard on him. I told him that he could show out if he wanted, but he wouldn't win. He replied, "I will win."

Something shifted in my spirit, and I realized that this was the wrong approach. I asked him to stay after class, and let him observe my well-behaved second-graders. I explained that I was teaching this class for those who wanted to learn, and that if he didn't, I probably couldn't change that. But if he did, and if he wanted to learn more than just the four-letter words he'd repeatedly written in his behavior journal that day, I would be thrilled to teach him. I explained to the second-graders that "my friend KamRon" was going to time them during the breathing exercise that starts my class, after the daily review of the rules, rewards and consequences. As previously stated, I've learned that the most challenging students usually love leadership roles and responsibility. He warmed up to me, despite continued challenges.

The principal approached me one day, as I was speaking with Kam at dismissal, and said, "I'm glad you're building a relationship with him. He missed more than one hundred days of school last year. When I'd call his mom, she told me she couldn't make him come."

"Who's paying for that phone he has?" I asked her. "Can't she, at least, take that?"

As I write about it now, however, I wonder if I'd let my own adolescent daughter run around the projects phoneless. Probably not. It's complicated.

There were two Camerons in my class that year, and one day when I was speaking with KamRon's teacher about his behavior, the teacher asked "Which one? The one with anger issues?"

On Fridays, my drama classes got free time outside if the weather was nice, provided they had completed the lessons and assignments for Monday through Thursday. On one of those Fridays, one of my incredibly sensitive seventh-graders refused to put his phone away when I asked him to. This held my class up from their free time, and KamRon was particularly frustrated. He asked me if he could take the phone and give it to me. I, somehow, misheard him when he asked if he could take the phone, (I thought he'd asked if *I* could take it) and responded in the affirmative.

KamRon, then, went over and grabbed the phone from my sensitive student, and attempted to give it to me. The sensitive student, let's call him Niko, tried to grab it back. KamRon, who was about 30 pounds heavier, responded, "We can do this the hard way if you want to," and began to wrestle with the student for the following two minutes, until another student pulled him off of Niko. I didn't have health insurance, at the time, so I no longer broke up fights where there was a chance that I might be hurt.

Understanding that KamRon meant well, as he was just trying to ensure that the class earned their free time, and help me out in the process, I did not refer this incident to the office, but mentioned it to the teacher and the behavioral specialist instead, checking in with Niko later to ensure he was okay. He was okay, and relayed that his phone was out because he was waiting for an update. I reminded him that this was not worth disrespecting my class. He agreed, and promised to do better in the future.

At the end of the fourth week of school, I left on another Friday to attend a wedding in Atlanta. While speaking with a friend at the Saturday wedding, who has five boy children, and is a school counselor, I shared some of the frustrations of my job.

She said, "You are there for a reason. Sometimes it's just about showing them there is another way to be." This stuck with me.

When I returned, the following Monday, KamRon seemed upset, but simply picked up his chair, and moved to sit next to me halfway through the lesson. I thought about my friend's words in that moment, realizing that my very presence seemed to calm him. Later, when we had broken up into smaller groups, and KamRon ended up across from me in the circle we had formed, I asked, "KamRon, do you need to sit next to me?" He didn't respond, but again, simply picked up his chair and moved to my side.

Two days later, when KamRon had a particularly challenging day, I had to ask the school behavioral specialist to remove him from the room after he refused to leave on his own. She seemed frustrated by this request. Wondering if KamRon's behavioral issues were a result of his academic ones, KamRon was asked to stay after class and told that I knew he had challenges with reading and writing, and was happy to help him with those, I also told him that I noticed that staff had a tendency to baby him. He was asked, in all honesty, if he felt he could not be expected to follow the same expectations as everyone else. He admitted that he could not, so I offered to allow him breaks inside of the room, after his third warning, as opposed to the time outside of the room expected by every other student after a third reminder.

I also offered to investigate his reading level, and offer him grade-level reading materials, with the caveat being that he had to agree to commit to thirty minutes a day of working with them. He was hesitant. I told him that I had failed the driving test five times, but now had my license, and that I didn't want to exercise thirty minutes a day, but that it is required for my body type. He finally agreed, reluctantly, looking me in my eye, at my request, shaking my hand, and saying, "deal."

In addition to the very challenging seventh-grade drama class I had that quarter, including KamRon, and a few other volatile personalities, I had an additional four students from a "self-contained" special education class. I started with five, but after sharing my frustration with my administrator, she removed one particularly challenging girl. For those who aren't familiar with education terminology, "self-contained" is the term for students who are so low academically, or challenging behaviorally, that they cannot function inside of a "general education" classroom. These students, as well as many in "gen pop" have "Individualized Education Plans," or I.E.P's, for short, that include their challenges, goals and specialized accommodations for instruction. One of these accommodations includes the requirement that these students be included in resource classes, including music, art, gym, and you guessed it — drama, so that they can have some social interaction with their peers. Two of these students had academic challenges, and were able to adjust to my class with ease. The remaining two had behavioral challenges that exacerbated the issues that are always present in the seventh grade already.

Two days following my conversation with KamRon, one of the behaviorally challenged special education students was making his notorious noises, while I was speaking with a student who'd gotten in trouble in the previous class. KamRon rose from his seat, and slapped the student who was making noises — hard.

Once I realized what had happened, I attempted to intervene, as Dante, the special education student who was slapped picked up a chair in retaliation. I guided Dante out of the room, asking him to take a break. When he returned, I asked him if he was okay, but he just said, "get out of my face," even though I was halfway across the room from him.

Another student, noting his aggressive disposition, exclaimed, "She's not in your face. You better not try to hurt my teacher. If you do, I'm coming for you."

Frustrated by the chaos, but trying to maintain calm, I proceeded to go on with my lesson. At one point, Dante, commented angrily to me, "You did nothing!"

It was true. I didn't know what to do, other than to write an office referral for KamRon later.

Ironically, in the class before, I'd had two visitors, one from the company I contracted with, who I'd also made aware of my frustrations, and one from a partner company who was attempting to get me a part-time assistant for my part-time position.

As I tried to maintain calm, and stick to my discipline system, which sent several students out of my room at their fourth warning (supposedly to my buddy room) the behavior specialist entered the room, with her own frustrations.

She told me that I couldn't continue to send students out, and that I needed to call parents instead. I told her that Dante was a toxin, aggravating the other students, to which she responded, "even when he's not here, you have problems."

I replied that it was still a difficult seventh grade. She reiterated that I needed to call some of their parents. I told her I'd called two the day before, but would call more. Then she said, "they say the reason they act up here is because you don't do anything, so they're bored." Then, to them, she added, "You guys don't behave like this anywhere else." I was deeply offended by this, as I pride myself on my thorough planning and student engagement.

Inviting her into the room, I said, "Ms. M says we don't do anything here. Who can say, to my face, that this is true? If it is, raise your hand." The students were silent, save for, to my surprise, KamRon, who slowly raised his hand.

As I thought about all of the work I had put into not only planning my lessons, but also the multiple compromises made with the volatile KamRon, I felt tears welling up in my eyes, and I couldn't stop the flood this time, as I'd managed to do the week before. I cried in front of my seventh-graders.

While waiting for their teacher to pick them up, I told them they could finish the warm-up game KamRon had complained we'd ended early, as I tried to transition into the lesson. I told them that we would need to use part of their Friday free-time to finish the lesson. They protested, but stopped when they realized I was really in tears.

That Monday, I'd given a Thank You card to their teacher for his support with their behavior thus far. Having been a classroom teacher, I was fully aware that he didn't have to intervene the way he had. Seeing the tears falling from my face as he arrived to pick them up, he said, "I'm too scared to ask." Then, although it was their lunch time, he instructed them to meet in his room.

That afternoon, I called Dante's number, as prompted by Miss M, and found that his father was quite understanding, and seemed willing to help, even as I apologized for having not called sooner, and for the fact that Dante had been slapped under my watch. I did explain, as I had, previously, to administration, and Ms. M., that if Dante couldn't follow my directions, it would be difficult for me to keep him safe. I listed, for example, a prior Friday when I had asked Dante to stay inside during our Friday free-time, but he had instead opted to follow us outside, and stay in an area where I couldn't possibly supervise. Similarly, when I'd told KamRon to stop imposing his vigilante justice, and let me deal with Dante instead, he'd said, in all honesty, "Every day you tell him to stop, but he never does." Dante's dad said he understood where I was coming from, and he even offered to stop by. I told him that the class was over, but now that I knew he was available, I'd definitely call on him in the future.

The next day, which happened to be a Friday, my seventh-graders brought letters of apology, and verbally apologized, one by one, as they entered the room. It was like something out of a movie. After they sat down, they also brought me their turned off phones one by one. A few minutes later, as we were processing the events of the day before, the principal entered. She told the students, and me, that she had sat in on their restorative circle that morning, and had come by to see if any of them wanted to apologize in person. I told her that most of them had written letters. This was, of course, all thanks to their super supportive classroom teacher.

KamRon spoke up, and said that he hadn't written a letter, but that he "had a few things to say." The principal asked him to speak, and he said he'd rather talk in private. I responded, "Since you were rude to me in public, I don't see why you can't apologize in public."

He did apologize, then, and he also said that he'd only raised his hand because he didn't understand the question. Wow! I'd allowed myself to get all worked up over a misunderstanding. He reiterated that he had a few other things to say, but he'd share them privately.

When I asked Kam, as I'd come to call him, about these sentiments later, he told me that he forgot what he wanted to say, but I put my arm around him as I thought about his challenges, remembering that it really wasn't personal. The fact that my colleagues had my back, and my students demonstrated that they did care ensured that I'd be back on Monday. I just needed a weekend to recover.

Monday was tough, but Mondays are usually tough. When students have been at home all weekend, often in dysfunctional situations, returning to the kind of structure and order offered by school is frequently both welcomed and difficult. Still, it was Wednesday that proved the most difficult for KamRon that week. He spent at least five minutes, spinning around in a chair, making it incredibly challenging for me to get to (let alone, through) my lesson. This was even after I'd asked the behavior specialist to take him out of the room for a spell; and this, only after he'd refused to take a break inside of the room.

When she did pull him for the determined ten minutes, he shouted, "I hope you get fired." I turned my phone to video mode when he returned, and began recording the ridiculousness, for no particular reason. I guess I thought that the idea that I might have proof of his behavior, that I could share, might curtail it. The behavior specialist/hall monitor asked if I'd called KamRon's parents. I admitted that I had not. KamRon often bragged that his mom wouldn't do anything, and I'd heard this sentiment echoed by my principal, the day she'd told me about her attempt to address the prior year's absences.

Nevertheless, I did call KamRon's mom that day. She told me that she was eight months pregnant, and seemed to explain this as her reason for not being able to get a hold on her teen. I told her that Kam told me that she wouldn't do anything, and in the most non-judgmental tone I could muster, also acknowledged that I am parenting an eighth-grader, who responds to the consequences of threatening to take her phone and social time. I repeated Dr. Phil's advice, "Every child has a currency."

KamRon's mom agreed to speak with him. The behavior specialist pulled him at the beginning of my class the next day as well. I wondered if she'd bribed him. Regardless, he did much better in my class for the rest of the week.

That Thursday, I asked Kam's language arts teacher what literacy level he was on, as I had once promised him to find out, in order to lend him books on his level. The teacher replied that this seventh grader was on kindergarten level the year prior.

At the end of the day, I heard KamRon's math teacher speaking with another student. She was telling her that regardless of what happened, she couldn't always retaliate. The student she was speaking to kept reiterating that, "he started it."

Another teacher joked with me, "He started it. I had to keep it going."
I laughed with the teacher, but asked the student who she was talking about. She said "KamRon." Speaking with the teacher afterwards, I found that Kam had thrown a pair of sneakers at the student. I told that teacher, and the teacher I'd laughed with earlier, "It's easy for us to say we would tell the teacher, but this

culture that they come from doesn't make that easy. It makes them prey."

I then asked Kam's language arts and math teachers what interventions were in place for him. His language arts teacher replied, "Whenever we bring him up, they just say 'we're just glad he's coming to school this year.'"

"Him coming to school is step one," I said, "Now, step two is, what are we going to do with him?"

Miraculously, as I was leaving that day, after tying up some loose ends in my classroom, I found Kam's teachers still outside. I joked, "Are you guys out here trying to save the world, one middle school student at a time?'

Kam's language arts teacher responded, seriously, "We have a meeting for KamRon tomorrow."

The next week, I hadn't checked back in about Kam's meeting, but noticed that he had been trying more. It was only a three day week, with two days off for professional development, and he was absent on Tuesday, but I did remember to check back in with him on Wednesday, when I had an unexpected free period, since my first class didn't show up when their teacher decided to keep them from my class as punishment for their behavior. I used that free period to pull Kam from his language arts class and asked if he'd been reading The Little Engine That Could book I'd lent him a couple of weeks prior. He admitted he hadn't, and I told him I needed him to, as we'd be out of school for an entire four days due to an upcoming holiday.

"I know you don't want anyone seeing you read <u>The Little Engine That Could</u>," I acknowledged. "Is there somewhere you can practice privately?"

He told me he could read it in his mom's room when she wasn't home, which told me more than I could have ever asked to know.

The following week, the company I was contracting with sent a fellow theatre teacher to shadow me. When she witnessed KamRon's challenges, and heard me speak about him, she asked, "Who is responsible?"

I replied that it was a combination of factors that get us to this point. One huge part of it is the government, who messed up a generation of kids with the "No Child Left Behind Act." It was a law that sounded good in theory, placing great responsibility on teachers for test scores, and emphasizing things like differentiation, rigor and engagement. These last three words were the current "buzz words" when I entered education full-time in 2010. The problem was it enabled poorly trained educational leaders, who weren't, necessarily, well-educated themselves to force feed children intense amounts of math and reading, but de-emphasized the need for socio-emotional elements like recess, art, music, and theatre, while also allowing teachers to neglect the less tested subjects of science and social studies. The result was a generation of students who dreaded learning, and perhaps, even more dismal, a decade of teachers who now dreaded teaching, due to an insane amount of bureaucracy and test preparation.

Add to this a couple of generations of poorly educated adults; as my dad once said, "We're not just teaching Be-Be's Kids. We're teaching Be-Be's grandkids," and you have a recipe for disaster. These new age inner city students are products of a surge of teenage parents, and a failed war on drugs that sent too many fathers, and mothers, out of their homes. An incredible number of parents were incarcerated for addiction issues, mostly caused by the stresses of poverty, instead of being offered counseling or treatment. We, who teach in the inner cities, are addressing severe trauma daily.

For example, one of my best students was having an unusually rough day one week, and behaving out of character. I kept her after class and asked her why she was so off. She explained that her cousin had been shot days prior, her electricity had been turned off, and was just turned back on, and that her mother was yelling at her that morning about her attitude. It's a lot.

I've often wondered myself how much of this poor education, and neglect, results from evil politicians who knew what they were doing, feeding the now much-discussed "school to prison pipeline," and how much of it was poorly educated educators, who, lacking critical thinking skills themselves, simply followed bad directions.

Either way, what is certain is that there have been many great ideas and theories in education that have not been backed by appropriate resources. One of these was the 1994 "Least Restrictive Environment" Law, which meant, in theory, that:

"A student who has a disability should have the opportunity to be educated with non-disabled peers, to the greatest extent appropriate. They should have access to the general education curriculum, or any other program that non-disabled peers would be able to access. The student should be provided with supplementary aids and services necessary to achieve educational goals if placed in a setting with non-disabled peers."

There is more to this law, which I won't bore you with here, but it is worth researching. Again, in theory, there aren't many of us, who believe in true education, who would argue with this law — *in theory.* However, the reality of its implementation meant that general educators, in most states, now became poorly trained, and improperly resourced, special educators as well.

The analogy I have often used to explain this implication to laymen is medicine. When we need a check-up, we go to our general practitioner, who can monitor our weight, blood pressure and general health indicators, but who, when faced with a specific condition, such as a heart or brain problem, appropriately, refers us to a specialist.

Under "Least Restrictive Environment," in most states, other than New York — where a special educator was paired in every classroom with the general educator — general classroom teachers charged with teaching 25 to 35 students how to read, write and multiply, now became responsible for creating differentiated lessons for students with anything from attention deficit hyper-activity disorder (ADHD) to dyslexia to severe emotional disorders.

In my analogy, this is equivalent to the general practitioner being responsible for things like brain surgery, heart surgery and cancer treatment, with only occasional consultations from specialists, as special educators are generally required to "push-in" an hour or two per week for each child, and "pull out" for another couple of hours, depending on the disability. This means they work with teachers in the classroom for an hour or two each week, and meet with each student, individually, for another hour or two.

In my several years of experience, special educators also have a very challenging time of meeting their required hours of "pull-out" and "push-in," due to the legalities of "Least Restrictive Environment" that require many more hours of staff and family meetings for our special educators who are required to make sure that they are meeting the demands of these individualized plans, without the (wo)manpower that would ensure their success.

In cities like Baltimore, where special needs, particularly socio-emotional needs, but also academic deficiencies, run rampant, this becomes an almost impossible, thus inevitably depressing and overwhelming task. These deficiencies are due in some part, to severe underfunding, and in larger part, to underaddressed trauma, which is also impacted by lack of funding. In addition, though studies have shown that special needs students, do in fact fare better, when placed in the general population, my experiences in teaching have shown that saner students who are forced to interact regularly with emotionally disturbed students, are compelled to adjust to their environment. This includes developing coping mechanisms such as mimicking the behavior of their emotionally challenged peers, for survival's sake.

One potential solution to this challenge is the model adopted in New York City of having a special educator in every classroom at all times.

One week, for example, my seventh-grade students were challenging as usual. While speaking to one of them, after school, I repeated some advice I often give to all of my students, "make sure you are reading outside of school."

She responded that she couldn't do this because she can't read. She clarified to say that she can't read anything other than baby books, and went on to state, "my dad is the opposite of me. He can read, but he can't understand. I can understand, but I can't read.

I AM EXASPERATED

I asked my student, let's call her Sofia, what her specific reading challenges were. She said that she didn't know, but told me that her prior year language arts teacher would. He was standing nearby, so I consulted him. Having become very familiar with these individualized education plans (I.E.P's) during my five years of full-time teaching I asked, does she actually have an identifiable learning disability, or does her I.E.P. simply state, "Specific Learning Disability" which, ironically, is the diagnostic code given to every student whose disability they can't really name. As a matter of fact, the code might as well be "Ambiguous Learning Disability" a.k.a. "We don't know exactly what this student's challenges are, but we are certain that there are special needs."

Her former teacher was able to utilize the technology on his phone to inform me that Sofia did, in fact, have a "Specific Learning Disability." As usual, I wasn't sure exactly how to address this issue.

I was talking with my student about a friend of mine who is dyslexic, but doing very well, when she said, "I have that too."

She also informed me, for the second time that year, that she has been told several times that she has bi-polar disorder, although she can not remember ever having any official diagnosis.

I am exasperated.

That Friday, there were at least three fights involving my four classes. It was supposed to be a "Free Friday" for all of my students who completed their Monday through Thursday assignments.

I spent at least thirty minutes outside with the fourth grade intervening with two girls who were calling each other names. I gave them both five-minute timeouts when they refused to heed my first three warnings about not yelling at me, or each other, and because they had each threatened to have an older sibling beat up the other. Even after the timeout, in which they, at least, stopped screaming and threatening each other, I found their mentalities so depressing and overwhelming, that I sent both of them off to play.

In my second class of seventh-graders, I had the audacity to turn around for an entire minute, after my students entered my class, in order to retape a detached word-search holder to the wall. In just that time, one seventh-grader had fallen to the floor, after some unfortunate turn of physics caused him to tumble from his seat, which had become entangled with another student's chair, which dislodged when the other student stood up. The displaced student lay on the floor, dramatically, for another minute, after I'd turned around before suddenly attacking the student he blamed for his embarrassing accident. The stricken student fought back, in turn, eventually throwing his attacker into a desk, causing the instigator's nose to bleed. I had to stop my class to write office referrals for both students, due to the injury. I could not, in turn, justify taking these students outside, per my original plan, so I had to improvise a new one on the spot.

After I finally dismissed the seventh grade, my second-graders arrived. The free time I had decided to give the ones that had completed the weekly assignments was thwarted by the news that there had been a fight. Their teacher asked me to implement the immediate consequence of having them sit out of my class.

Because my second-graders came to me after their lunch period, half of them had to use the restroom, so I played music, and allowed the rest of the class to dance, as the teaching assistant and I allowed them to go, two at a time, using the two passes I was allotted. By the time every student who claimed they needed to use the restroom had used the facilities, we had 15 minutes left for them to play outside.

During part of the alleged twenty-minute break I have between my third and final class, I went to lie down in the pillow-filled section of the "Mindfulness" room, for five minutes, as I was already overwhelmed. As I lay, I heard one of our behavioral specialists addressing the parent of one of my sixth-graders, who should have been attending my final class of the day. This student and I had developed a friendly kickball rivalry on our free Fridays, but today, he was being sent home because he'd gotten into a fight with one of our ESOL (English as a Second Language) students who can barely speak English. This fight was, apparently, the result of that student cursing at him, and calling him "gay."

"Who taught him these words, as his first means of communication?" I wondered.

I introduced myself to the mom of my sixth-grade fighter, who was coming to pick up her student. She explained to our behavioral specialist that she is a housecleaner at a hotel, and the only English speaker. As a result, she believes that our Spanish speaking students probably do pick on our English speakers, or at least, know what they're saying. This is the experience at her job.

I am exasperated.

Nevertheless, having risen from my pile of pillows, and after taking this opportunity to introduce myself to my student's mom, I tell her that I have her second-grader in one class, and her sixth-grader in another. Her sixth-grader shares my father's name. Her second-grader shares part of my name.

The behavioral specialist laughs, and says we must have been meant to meet.

Our sixth-grade fighter gets sent home, with one impending day of in-school suspension. I put my arm around him, and tell him, honestly, that I will miss him in kickball.

Before we go outside, I spend a few minutes lecturing my students about the responsibility of modeling appropriate behaviors and language, and provide them an opportunity to comment, using a "popcorn" method, where one student speaks, then calls on another student to do so. I tell them my "hypothesis" is that my predominantly Spanish-speaking student learned these "fighting words" from his peers, probably not knowing that they are fighting words.

I try to believe that my Black students "popcorning" to only other Black students, and not to my White and Latinx students, is coincidental. I am a teacher, though, so I must question my own conditioning, and potential bias. I'm pretty sure that these choices were on purpose. The question becomes, is it worth addressing now, or next week, since this incident happened on a Friday? As I reflect, over the weekend, I remember that there was, in fact, one White and Latinx student who was called on twice, I have one less battle to fight.

That settled, let's return to the law of "Least Restrictive Environment." Having returned to contracting, many of the protections I enjoyed through the system had been removed. As aforementioned, as a theatre enrichment, or "resource" teacher, I was sometimes given classes that included a small class of special education students who had been identified with such significant needs that they had been placed in a "self-contained" classroom during the school day. As part of their I.E.P.'s, these students had their resource classes with the general population so that they could get some socialization skills, and experience, with peers of a similar age.

Again, while this sounds appropriate in theory, without an extra educator, or assistant, who is skilled in special education, these classes often become incredibly difficult to manage. Many of my students mean well when they threaten each other. They are more frustrated than I am when I am not able to speak or deliver instruction due to students who insist on making noises and being disruptive throughout the class, and who refuse to adhere to our behavior system; students who legally aren't even required to adhere to our behavior system, because they don't have the mental capacity, or ability to reason in the same way as their peers. The behaviors are not always defiant. Sometimes they are compulsive. I try, but it is challenging to explain this to an entire class of seventh-graders.

I beg, "Please don't touch him. Please don't hit him."

"Then ask him to be quiet," they plead.

I have, and he won't. As I try to console a student who is so agitated by the behavior, that she is shaking, I realize I am shaking as well. I take a deep breath to try to keep the tears that have formed in my eyes from falling.

"Maybe we should just do our 8-8-8 breathing," another student suggests.

"We don't do the breathing on Friday," the shaking student beside me retorts.

Although it is a "Free Friday," we can not go outside today because it is too cold, so I am planning to take a vote on whether students will go to centers or play a game of Drama Jeopardy. Teaching twenty drama classes a week has taught me that trying to talk over students will result in me losing my voice, so I am waiting. It has been twenty minutes.

When my special education students return from a break the other students have convinced them to take, they note my visible frustration, and one convinces the other to go work on a word-search in my library. I am finally able to begin my class.

SOME CONSEQUENCES

In the first quarter of my most challenging school year, one of my seventh grade classes also incorporated a small class of special needs students, making it my most difficult. In the second quarter it was the fourth grade that had an additional class joining them. The problems, however, were similar in both cases. For example, there was one student, I'd been told by his teacher, "will not sit in a whole group [of students]."

For the first week, that student sat in my library, eating snacks. It was messy, and annoying, but, then, in our second week, he had begun to wander the class. He didn't cause any problems, other than the obvious one. If he didn't have to follow my directions, why should anyone else? On that day, which was the third day of the second week in the quarter, and the last day of Thanksgiving break, another student from his class decided she didn't need to sit in my class circle as well. They took their cues from each other.

Additionally, there was another student from the self-contained class, who apparently flipped his middle finger at one of the more challenging students in the, what would be referred to as, "general education" class. The student in the general education class was already volatile, but because I called his mother on the first day, was also, generally manageable, until he was activated by the child who flipped him off. Let's call him Isaac.

Twice that week, when I turned my back to these students for twenty seconds, Isaac had flipped off my easily-angered student, we'll call him Michael, resulting in Michael attacking Isaac. Both times, Isaac flipped completely out, then left the room. The first day, he tore down a poster on the inside of my door. The next day he destroyed the outside door covering my sixth-graders had been working on for six days. I tried to remain calm through all of this, but my class asked me if I was upset about it, and I admitted that I was. This upset continued into my next class of seventh grade, who I had to explain my attitude to, before my executive director walked in for my "formal observation."

Fortunately, for me, that seventh grade was one of my best classes, so not only did they understand, but they also turned on their very best behavior for my observation.

I wrote an office referral for Isaac, while attempting to recover from my rough day in our school's "Mindfulness" room. Before leaning back on the pile of pillows to write, I consulted with one of our two behavior specialists, "So let me ask you, but I'm going to do it anyway, will anything come of me writing this referral? I know he has an I.E.P."

Many of the Individualized Education Plans for our special needs students state that they cannot be subject to the same consequences as our general education students, due to their disabilities. Try explaining that to your average fourth-grader.

Anyway, the specialist replies, "We can't do much [due to the I.E.P], but we can give him detention." I reply, "I'll take it." Some consequence is better than no consequence.

He writes the detention down for the following week, which is the next possible detention slot, and relays it to the teacher. I hear her say, "He's not going to understand."

The behavior specialist replies that the other behavior specialist, who monitors detention in their room, will explain it to him. Before getting up from my pile of pillows, I thank him for having my back.

THIRTY MINUTES A DAY

I was working through one of the Oprah/Chopra free 21-day meditation series. It was called "Making Every Moment Matter," and it was all about time. There really are no coincidences. I talk a lot about time, in my teaching, because I am so concerned about the time that we waste. Sometimes, I'll do an exercise with my students, where I ask them how much time they waste on behavior. I'll then average their estimates, and calculate how much of their education they don't receive. In my thirteen years of educating in Baltimore, that average seems to be about half of their instructional time. This frightens me. These days, I often share with my students that I am deeply concerned about statistics that show many of our high school seniors graduating with only a sixth grade education. I explain that they are no less intelligent than their peers in other districts. They simply receive less instruction and practice time due to these consistent disruptions.

I shared with them a quote I read in <u>Think and Grow Rich: A Black Choice</u> where the author states, "The moment a person's education makes itself known is through their communication, be it written or verbal. However, thirty minutes a day of reading, and serious study, can offset even the poorest education." Actually, I shared it with them time and time again, as one educational text said that it takes nine times of hearing a particular piece of information for students to remember. We broke the statement down to: *People decide how smart they think you are when they hear you speak, or read what you've written. However, no matter how behind you may fall, you can make up for it with serious and sustained educational effort.*

We all know, or have heard of someone, who educated themselves from prison. As much as I admire teachers, I do believe this theory that people can educate themselves. I share it with my students because I find it heartbreaking that even those who show up every day, and do what they are supposed to do, may lose up to fifty percent of their instructional time, due to time lost to behavior management, even given a highly competent teacher.

I encourage those who want to go to college, start their own businesses, and/or have careers, to read and study outside of the classroom, because they can't possibly be getting all that they need inside of the toxic environment that is most inner city schools.

Again, this breaks my heart. Reader, you have no idea the extent to which this is true, but I do my best to maximize the learning time inside of my classroom, and I cling to the hope that a few of them will remember this advice.

PASSING THE TORCH

It was the week before Thanksgiving break, and I was so tired. It was taking everything in me to even write this paragraph. I did it only because I knew so many teachers were feeling the same way, and on this night, I wanted to remind them that they are not alone.

A week, and a day before writing this, I had come home and told my mother that I didn't want to return on Monday. We'd just ended the first quarter, and I'd never felt less inspired by a group of students, and less motivated, generally, as I did then.

Fortunately, we had a professional development that Saturday. A few things happened there. First, one of my program directors acknowledged that I was teaching in the toughest school they had, but she went on to say, "If she [meaning me] has behavior problems, I don't know about them," and, "One thing I can say is that those students are engaged." She went on to share with our staff that my students rapped their rules to the tune of a popular rap song. I felt valued for the first time in a long time. Second, another director spoke about the very real challenges that we face in Baltimore, and the need for culturally responsive programming.

Third, the teacher who had shadowed me a week prior to this development, spoke with me afterwards, and asked, "Have you ever thought about mentoring teachers? I think you'd be really good at that."

I replied, "From your mouth to God's ears."

I have to admit, I've gotten really good at teaching our toughest children, but it's taken its toll on me. I don't want to give up on the students the world has already given up on, but I am burning out. I told her I feel like a very low candle that keeps being relit. The idea of teaching teachers appeals to me, for this very reason, I won't be able to take it much longer, but maybe I can share what I have learned. Perhaps I can pass on the skills I have acquired as my final gift to our most challenging schools.

The buildup I received that weekend was enough to convince me to return that Monday to the start of a new quarter. In my theatre classes, I was assigned to the same four grades, in the same order: fourth, seventh, second, and sixth. I quickly discovered that the behavior problems I had before were reversed. In the prior quarter, my elementary classes had been easy, and my middle school classes had been challenging. This quarter, my middle school classes were cool, but my elementary classes were hard.

There was something else though. I had some talented students that quarter. They made sure I knew that they were talented on day one. In my seventh grade class there were a few girls who could dance, and choreograph, along with a boy who could both beatbox and dance. In my sixth grade, there were three girls who were visual artists. I put those students to work immediately. The seventh-graders saved the showcase I was supposed to present for the end of the quarter. When I asked, on a Tuesday, if anyone could be ready to present by that Friday, one girl spoke up, offering her friend as a potential partner. The friend later declined, after asking who would be in the audience. I told her, I thought it would be grades four through eight, and some parents. I asked the first girl if she was still willing to perform, and she said, "I'll do it by myself if I have to. I'm not scared."

I commended her for her courage, and by Thursday, she had convinced three girls to join her in both choreographing and performing a routine to Andra Day's "Rise Up."

Meanwhile, I asked the student that I had learned had a talent for beatboxing if he would contribute to the showcase. He told me, "I like to beatbox, but I love to dance." So I asked him to choreograph something school-appropriate as well, after he demonstrated his skills.

Between those students, and the "rap of rules" my first quarter students were already familiar with, I suddenly had a fall showcase worthy of presentation.

There was, however, a slight scare when one of my more stubborn seventh-graders refused to follow a simple rule, later that week, of putting her book bag in the designated spot. I told my students that I could not "reward bad behavior," and that until she followed my directions, I could not begin my class, thus reducing their rehearsal time, which meant that they might not be ready to perform by the end of the week.

The students who had followed my directions were irate, since they had worked so hard on their routine. The student who first volunteered to perform even threatened to call her mom to advocate for her ability to perform. Some students debated whether I even had the power to keep them from performing. They argued that they could probably convince another teacher to allow them to. I calmly stated that if that happened, I would probably resign, as it would be a sign that they didn't need to follow my directions. I apologized to the affected students, and finally agreed to let them practice their dance in class, explaining that if the stubborn student did not adhere to my directive, I still would not allow them to perform in the showcase, as it would send the wrong message that she didn't have to follow our class norms.

I checked in with my ego to make sure that this wasn't just a power trip, and having done so, decided that it truly was in the best interest of the students. If this one stubborn student refused to follow my directions on week one, it would cause a delay in every class hereafter, and that, I believed, wasn't fair to my class. As I'd later explain to my elementary student's mother, the bookbags can present a safety hazard, as they sometimes presented an obstacle to movement. I also didn't want anyone tripping on them, or getting upset if someone bumped into them during a movement exercise.

I stared out of my classroom window, in sorrow, for at least fifteen minutes, imagining how I would apologize to the person coordinating the assembly, who I'd been working with.

With fifteen minutes left in class, the stubborn student's backpack finally made it the designated area. I heard her say something to the effect of, "I'm not going to let my friends suffer." Another student asked me, "Are you happy now?" I assured her that I was very happy.

My students went on to rock their showcase!

THE ART OF THE PARENT CALL

My Facebook status the Monday after Thanksgiving 2017 read:

I was totally prepared for end-of-holiday craziness today, but it was actually a good day. I know this because:

1. My seventh-grade class asked to stay just a few minutes into their lunch to finish their presentations.

2. The fourth-grader who gave me the blues for the first two weeks skipped his lunch entirely, to sit in on my next class — for the second time.

3. The sixth-graders asked to work just a little bit beyond the afternoon announcements to finish their presentations.

4. Two of my former seventh-graders asked if they could skip P.E. to sit in on my class tomorrow.

5. It also didn't hurt that a few of my former fourth-graders commented on how much younger I look. Rest is an elixir.

The next day, however, Quentin, the same fourth-grade student who had stayed after in my class, twice, flipped out, and threw a few chairs. Despite the fact that he forewarned me twice before throwing any furniture, first stating "Don't mind me, Miss Asia. My mom gave me one pill this morning instead of two," and later, premeditatively warned, "I'm about to throw this chair," I was dismayed and discouraged.

I'd already called this student's mom once. I called her again on Tuesday, sharing that he'd had a great day on Monday, and I hated to be calling again with bad news. I told her what he'd shared about the pills, but I didn't share the part where he'd told me he went to the mental hospital over the holiday. He offered this revelation after rapper Logic's song, named after the suicide hotline, had shuffled its way onto my "school playlist."

When I asked my elementary behavior specialist's opinion about this admission, he suggested it was most probably a lie, but did suggest I bring it up to his mom. We make so many decisions each day, and week, as teachers, that all I can say is, I decided not to include this important disclosure with his mom that day. If he was telling the truth, I didn't want to get him in trouble with his mother for sharing such intimate information. In retrospect, I probably should have followed up with the school counselor at the very least. These kinds of regrets are why I always say teaching is a very humbling profession. There are so many opportunities to get it wrong.

So maybe I share some responsibility, due to this omission, that this same student threatened me, two days later, when I told him to leave a student he'd been picking on alone. Might things have gone differently if I'd made someone else aware of his fragile mental state? I don't know. I will add, however, that I had also documented various other instances with this student, and that many of us were aware that he was deeply troubled.

Anyway, on the day in question, I reprimanded him for making fun of another student.

"Shut the f$*% up before I bang you in your face!" he screamed.

It was only the second time I've been threatened in this fashion in over twenty years of teaching. The last time, the principal told the young man that student conduct guidelines suggested he should be expelled due to the threat, but he'd let me make that call. That student, ultimately apologized, and stayed in school.

This time, I was told, by the secondary behavior specialist, who I'd grown to love and respect, that she could push for an in-school suspension.

Later, the primary behavior specialist relayed that the student had actually been suspended for three days. Both he, and the other behavior specialist, were proud of this result. However, it was later admitted to me that he'd only received this severe consequence because he "went after" the student I'd tried to protect, again, following my class.

At the end of the day, as I was standing outside after dismissal, his mom asked me if I was planning to leave. I replied in the affirmative, and she asked me to stay, just for a moment. A few minutes later, she returned with her son, and she insisted that he apologize. He said, "I'm sorry for throwing chairs in your room."

"And?" she interrogated.

"It won't happen again," he promised.

I believed mom's sincerity, but it would mean more, coming from him, if we hadn't had a similar conversation just the day before.

That same week I decided to call the parent of a student in the same grade, let's call him Craig. Craig refused to put his coat and bookbag in the assigned area every day, and for the most part, I'd let it go. Today, however, he also decided it was okay to crawl around the floor during my class. Both the refusal to correctly place the coat and bookbag, and the crawling, can be dangerous in my drama class, as we frequently move around quite a bit. When I asked Craig to stay after class to contact his mom about the matter, he threw a fit, and attempted to escape through the classroom door. I stood in the doorway to block him from leaving, as he both pushed and punched me. I asked my next class of seventh-graders to bear witness to his aggression. When his teacher arrived, a bit late, as usual, I told him that I was keeping Craig for a parent call.

"Be careful with that parent," he warned. "She isn't always lucid, and she's been known to go off on teachers."

"Well, that's just great," I thought, but I thanked him aloud.

One of my next classes of seventh-graders offered to find Craig's eighth-grade sister, as the number I had for his mother wasn't working.

As I blocked Craig from leaving my room, his sister showed up. I asked her to call her mom for me and she said "I'm not gonna lie, he does come home every day saying you've been 'getting smart' with him."

This didn't shock me, as Craig had been exclaiming the whole time I'd been holding him that he was going to tell his mom about how I'd "been getting smart" with him.

It was, probably, a stroke of luck that when Craig's mom showed up at the school, approximately an hour later, I had a very small class of well-behaved seven seventh-graders who promised me that I could leave them alone, for a moment, as I went to speak with Craig's mother, who claimed she couldn't climb the stairs due to an injured leg. I asked the behavior specialist, in the hall, to keep an eye on them while I went to the office.

I told the parent, upon my descent, that Craig refused to follow basic directions, like putting his coat and bookbag in the designated area, but that he also insisted on crawling on the floor that day, and that this was unacceptable, as it posed a safety hazard.

Fortunately, she understood. Her only question was why was he still in the general population, when she had been told that he would be placed in special education. I explained to her that even the special education students had been placed in my class, due to individualized education plans that dictated that these students should be placed in resource classes for the sake of socialization, despite the fact that I have no assistance, as a drama teacher. Her son, however, was not in special education, but I wasn't sure why. She definitely seemed to understand that this wasn't my fault, or my problem.

She also seemed clear that my behavior concerns were not about my ego, or the fact that I couldn't handle her child, but rather, about the safety of her son and his classmates.

She reprimanded her son, and told him that he needed to follow my directions in the future. Not only did I never have a problem with that student again, but every day he'd ask me, "Did I have a good day?"

When I responded in the affirmative, he'd reply, "Tell my teacher," and I did.

POSITIVE PARENT CALLS

I love making positive parent calls. A particular one that stands out was calling with a praise report to the mom of a student I had to ask for support earlier in the quarter. Her son had been chosen by another student to partner on a rap, for an upcoming school performance, that they wrote and half-memorized in less than two days.

Back before having either student in my class, I had to stop my car at the end of the school's driveway because her son was pummeling this writer. I only knew the victim because he'd introduced himself to me prior; and I wanted to break up the fight — but doing so, effectively, would have meant pushing her son into the street. As I approached, I told the student, "I don't want to push you into the street."

He replied, "If you push me into the street, me and you will be fighting."

This made me sad, as I would later relay to a friend, and then the behavior specialist, "I forgot there is no code anymore. It used to be that young men did not hit women and elders."

I was deeply concerned about having this student in my class that quarter, and I was grateful for his mother's support when

I finally called. I admit I delayed my call because I thought his behavior might be indicative of a lack of parental support. So, when I called that day, and told her that not only had he memorized half of his lines, but that he'd also helped select a track for his rap, and a separate track for the rap included in the one page script I'd written for the other seven participating students, I was proud.

"He's a leader when he wants to be," I said.

"Yes, he's very smart," she agreed. "I just don't know why he has to show off all the time."

"Many performers are show-offs," I laughed. "I'm just glad to see him using his gift constructively and creatively."

She asked me what time the performance would be the next week, told me that he'd already shared that it was happening, and promised to attend.

"I look forward to meeting you," I said, after sharing, "If I can call about a problem, I'm always happy to call when they are doing something great."

I'm often overwhelmed by the love I have for my daughter. I sometimes wonder if other parents really love their offspring as much as I do. The thought of it kind of wows me! I've come to the realization that most do, even if we don't know how to parent perfectly much of the time. I dedicated that showcase to all of the parents who love their children, as much as I love my child. It takes a village!

ON CLASS SIZE

The next quarter I was blessed to have two middle school classes that happened to be very low in class size. Generally, I had about ten students in my seventh grade class at that time. It was a small class, anyway, but several of the students were enrolled in a separate drama class sponsored by a local theater. The teacher for this class was someone I'd met before, when interviewing for a documentary about teaching, for a progressive agency I'd become acquainted with. At the time of my interview, she'd just been released from a full-time position teaching drama, because she failed to pass some new, and ridiculously bureaucratic measure, called an S.L.O., or Student Learning Objective. It was an arbitrary measure for most teachers, but was particularly useless when applied to resource teachers who were, generally, responsible for teaching every child in the school.

Like many of the new initiatives the city had adopted, it had been poorly implemented, and more poorly modeled, leading to the demise of many, otherwise capable, teachers. In my last two years of teaching, I had also struggled with the latest attempt to hold teachers accountable for student outcomes.

Anyway, this teacher had now accepted a position as an ESOL (English as a Second Language) instructor, but prior to my hiring, had been promised the opportunity to teach some theatre. It just so happened that the local theatre program she'd worked to invite for a series of playwriting workshops coincided with my theatre class, so yeah, I ended up with ten students. It was incredibly awesome. I'd been able to develop the type of relationships in this class that are actually effective at this adolescent stage.

My sixth grade was also, uncharacteristically, small. As a result of low enrollment for that grade in the school, I had been gifted with this anomaly of thirteen, or so students.

These two small classes allowed me to better tolerate my larger classes of fourth and second-graders. My first period of fourth-graders was particularly difficult. This class of twenty-nine included five students from the "self-contained" special education class. Unfortunately, these I.E.P.'s did not include any additional support, personnel-wise, for my class. Additionally, there were four or more ESOL students who were pushed into my drama class, anywhere from halfway to three-quarters through our daily time, after their specialized instruction. It was challenging enough to have these students, who were just learning English, in a theatre class, but it added a layer of difficulty to have them coming in late each day.

It made for a frustrating scenario, no matter how talented I considered myself to be. Add to that one emotionally disturbed child — who still managed to hang in the general education class, but who had thrown chairs twice, and threatened me — and it was a whole lot.

A few weeks into the new quarter, I was over it all. That Monday, I didn't want to go back. However, my small classes redeemed my love for teaching, as we were able to have fun together.

Those smaller classes were actually able to get through, what would usually be, a week's worth of lesson plans in a couple of days, due to many fewer interruptions that I am used to, to the point where I had to improvise additional material for them by Thursday each week. Organizing each week into a unit with the four different grades I taught each quarter is what kept me sane.

All of my students got free-time on Fridays,* if they had finished the week's assignments/curriculum, but I was particularly impressed that last week, by the way my seventh-graders spent their free-time.

After my fourth-grade class on Friday, I was spent. I had already had to walk into the hallway at one point, just to breathe and gain my bearings. Then I was told that the colleague who usually takes some of my seventh-graders during the second period was absent, and I would have them all. I spent another few minutes with my back against the wall and my eyes closed, in the hallway, just trying to prepare.

At the beginning of my class, I told the seventh-graders the truth, that those fourth-graders had taken everything I had in me that day, but since they had earned their free time, I just needed them to find something quiet to do.

As I set up a workstation to create some bulletin board material, one student asked if she could help me. I moved another desk from the game center to the back of the room, where I could monitor the most students, so she could help me. Another two students sat in a far corner of the front of the room playing the game *Memory*. Five of the boys sat in the corner, opposite me, playing video games in a circle they had created, but bonding. Two girls sat behind us, in the art center, drawing and coloring; and in front of us, in another corner of the room, five, or six more girls sat in a circle, first singing and dancing, then, later, freestyling over a beat.

I looked around the room, some fifteen students, and thought, "this is what education *should* look like."

*Note about the "Free Fridays:" As a contract resource teacher, students were not graded for my class, so this free-day became both a behavior management tool and an academic incentive. I found that students were more productive with the promise of a potential free day than if I attempted to teach every day. They knew that if they wasted time Monday through Thursday, they would lose time on Friday. If I got behind in the lessons, I could make them up then. It also helped account for the many short-weeks during the year, with holidays and professional development days. Finally, I was afforded very little paid planning time, only twenty-minutes a day, so the free days gave me time to catch my breath, build relationships, and create materials.

WHAT'S MY MOTIVATION?

One of the best quotes I've ever read about writing is, "I don't like writing. I like having written." Agreed. So, here I am again, showing up to the page.

Last week, my upper level drama students engaged in one of my favorite lessons. I love teaching drama (although I also miss teaching language arts and social studies) because it is so applicable to life.

This particular lesson teaches students about objectives, tactics, obstacles and motivation. I guide students through definitions and examples of each of these terms, using familiar characters and stories, then model my expectation for them of creating their own short or long-term goals, including tactics, potential obstacles and motivation, by sharing my own. Students are then asked to complete a template where they list one personal objective, their tactics for achieving it, potential obstacles to the fulfillment of their dreams and a motivation strong enough to overcome the challenges they will face.

My example, after asking for student input, looks like:

> Objective: To teach a safe and fun class where students
> learn and get smarter

Tactics: Teaching, and review of, routines and
procedures for safety, incorporating games
and fun exercises

Obstacles: Disruptive behavior, difficult parents (the
latter is an example of student input)

Motivation: To contribute to a fair world where
students have equal opportunities to
be successful, including great teachers
and education

I give my students, who are usually divided into groups (half at "learning centers" and half doing the lesson and exercise) about 15 minutes to complete their template and then another ten minutes, or so, to share their responses.

The interesting thing is that, although my students do not receive a grade for my class, they almost always complete my work, and most are eager to share their responses. I've found that most people really enjoy talking about themselves.

Anyways, after completing the assignment, my fourth-graders were eager to share their work. One of my most challenging students, Quentin, said that his objective was to get his father back home, and that his tactics would be to beg his mother, since he is "spoiled," and usually gets whatever he wants. He went off on a tangent, however, when he got to his obstacles, and I told him that they had nothing to do with his objective. I asked him to listen to a few more examples, to see if he could identify where he'd gone off course.

After a few more students had shared, the challenging child said, "My obstacle is that my father has 10 years, and won't be home until I'm twenty."

Before I could respond, another student added "My dad will be home when I'm twenty-one."

A third student added, instantly, "My dad's in jail too."

My face dropped.

"All of your fathers are in prison?" I asked, incredulously. They each responded in the affirmative. Class was ending. I asked my students in centers to clean up, and hugged each of the students who had just shared obstacles that left me dumbfounded. It was all I had to offer, but when one of the students said, "Can I have another hug? Squeeze me tighter." I knew that it was enough, at least, to get them through another day.

I thought about my many personal objectives, including leaving this profession, this population, and even this country; and realized that, in this moment, there was nowhere else I could possibly be.

ON CULTURE AND CLIMATE

In January of 2018, I received an award from my agency for "Best Classroom Management." The program manager said that she felt "warm and loved" when she entered my room. This meant the world to me, on several accounts. First, I had not received an award since college. Second, I would have never known the program manager felt that way, as she usually seemed a bit stoic when she observed. Third, this was one of the most demanding schools in one of the toughest neighborhoods in Baltimore, so I was very proud.

Still, I had to share this award with the staff at my school, which took careful measures to create a behavior system that was both idealistic and realistic in its implementation. Let me explain. The system for behavior management at the school was as follows: the first time a student was out of order, we gave them a reminder of expectations. We're not supposed to use the word "warning," *reminder* was preferred, but I often forgot this, and used the word "warning" I had become accustomed to. I'm not perfect.

The second time a student defied classroom "norms," you asked the student to come sit next to you, and would have a quick conversation reminding them of expectations. This part is probably the most idealistic, as it's not always possible to interrupt the lesson, but even the proximity of having a student who needs support sit next to you is helpful.

The third time a student was disruptive, you'd ask them to "sit out" in the room, somewhere that you had designated. I had a desk set up next to a cabinet in the room, which provided just a little bit of privacy for the student. I had posted "cool down" strategies in that area.

The fourth time a student didn't follow the rules, they were given a behavior reflection sheet that they had to take to an assigned "buddy room." The reflection sheet was their pass, and they could return to class once it was filled out. There were two versions of the reflection sheet, which were provided by the school. One sheet had a space to draw pictures of what happened for students who couldn't read well. The second sheet asked for more writing-based responses. The only time I needed to write office referrals then, for the most part, was if students got into a serious fight, or if they chose not to adhere to the system, for example, refusing to take a break or fill out the behavior form.

We also had two behavior specialists, one who primarily managed the upper grades, and another who primarily managed the lower grades. They were both very good at their jobs, clearly cared for the students, and were supportive of me, and my colleagues as educators. Early in the year, there were times when one of them had to remind me to call parents when I had a repeated issue. The school also provided me with a list of numbers and addresses for the parents of each student. On a few occasions, I used these addresses to visit the homes of offending students. Most of the addresses were outdated, and I don't think I actually got one right that year, but the attempt helped me to remember the challenges of transient students, while also illustrating to them that I was serious enough to go to such extreme measures as seeking out their residences.

In order to drop the rate of out-of-school suspension, the school where I worked had also created structures for after school detention and in-school suspension. When I felt a student was particularly out of control, I was able to request that they serve a detention. This is important to note because, not long prior, I had engaged in an online discussion with a principal in an educator's group about the role of administration. She told me that her district did not provide for consequences like detention. I responded that while I am a huge proponent of the restorative practices many schools are now pushing, I find them most successful when coupled with fair and consistent consequences. I was surprised to later find out that we actually worked in the same district. Where was the disconnect, I wondered?

The school used an online behavior management system for their general education teachers called *Classroom Dojo*. Students could earn or lose points for specific goals and behaviors. Students who earned 80% or more of the expected points were invited to a monthly incentive. The incentive might include a party, sports activity, or a field trip.

Having switched contracting agencies that year, the executive director of my new agency gave all of us a small book about classroom management for resource teachers: <u>Classroom Management for Art, Music, and PE Teachers</u> by Michale Linsin.

Although I had been teaching drama, off and on, for years, this was an excellent, comprehensive read that made me a much better teacher. She didn't insist that we read it. She didn't demand that we discuss it. She simply provided it as a resource, and it proved to be an excellent one.

While I took pride in my award, it was only working with an effective team that allowed me to be as successful as I was. I should also stress, as you have probably noted by now, that I still had bad moments and bad days.

I can take credit for the fact that I reviewed my rules, routines and procedures with my students regularly. I tried not to bore them with the review, so sometimes I'd use different voices, or even sing them. One class, that year, challenged me to rap the rules, so I wrote them to the tune of a popular rap song, at the time, "Bodak Yellow" by Cardi B.

Lyrics for this version are on the following pages. Those in caps represent the words that students would say in unison. After a few times of me reciting it, students began to take turns reading the main lines.

Rule #1 is Respect Yourself
If I videoed
recordings of yourself in class
Yo, WOULD YOU BE PROUD TO SHOW

Rule #2
Keep hands and feet to self
THEY WON'T BE BUGGING YOU
we use kind language,
so you'll feel respected
SO, GET COMFORTABLE

Rule #3
You respect me
I speak, you listen
eyes on me
follow directions the first time
YOU KNOW WE CANNOT WASTE THIS TIME
you gotta question
raise your hand
there's lots of you
one me. Be kind.

Finally —
if you got this far
here goes number 4
respect the space, time, money, energy
your class is who it's for
leave the room just as you found it
maybe even better 'cause if you see trash on the floor
students, YOU KNOW WHERE IT GOES

135

Rewards include your free time
Fridays should be yours for sure
Did you follow all those rules thru 3
and Respect Number 4
Once a month
there's an incentive
tell me if you will be there
disrespect all of these rules
and you won't be there
I swear

Consequences
1st: reminder
2nd: come sit next to me
remind you of expectations
MIND YOU WHERE YOU'RE S'POSED TO BE
3rd time: Please sit in reflection
COME BACK WHEN YOU'VE WHAT YOU NEED
and the 4th go to the buddy room
and fill out the
REFLECTION SHEET
After that you lose free time
long as it took to write this rhyme
and if you fight
you're outta sight
office referrals
Will be typed
or maybe written out by hand
You get the Point?

WE UNDERSTAND!

My students loved taking turns rapping the lead on this. Sometimes we did it over the instrumental, but it helped them to remember the expectations, for sure.

I also spent the first week or two, in my ten-week class, just going over what correct behavior looks like. I gave them specific scenarios and one of the rules like, "Respect each other when entering the classroom," or, "Respect the Teacher during the warm-up game." They also created skits, after my modeling one, and us practicing one together, about what each scenario looks like when it's done well, and when it's not. They love role-playing bad behavior! I also had five "centers" in the room, and I explicitly taught and modeled how to behave in each of the centers, including using "library voices" in the centers while I worked with smaller groups.

One critical factor in creating a positive climate and culture is building relationships.

We were in the middle of the second week of the third quarter. I love the part where the most challenging students have been won over. The ones who don't always experience success in school get to experience success in my class, and they start to tell me their stories.

One day, due to a fluke in the schedule, I had my eighth-grade class for two hours. Their assignment was to interview each other, and then present their findings in front of the class, so that I could get to know them, and they could get to know each other better.

Most students did well, but there were four students who, for one reason or another, did not complete the assignment. In one of my early teaching texts, <u>Teach Like a Champion</u>, there was a philosophy called "no opt-out" that I have adopted for the most part. Since I had the extra time, I asked these four students to redo the assignment while the other students received a break. Two of the students just walked out in response. One hid in the room. I calmly called the office to inform them about the students who had left, and sat down with the one student who hadn't run from the assignment. I interviewed him myself, and took notes. When I was finished, I asked, "Now was that so bad?" He admitted that it wasn't.

The student who went into hiding in the room appeared after I called the office. He didn't want those problems. I interviewed him as well.

Finally, the two students who had simply left the room returned on their own. I admonished them for leaving, then, interviewed them both individually. One of the questions I asked was, "When's your birthday?" and it turned out that one of their birthdays was the day before mine. I told him that. The other student's birthday happened to be the day after one of my three best friends, and I told him how much I love Sagittariuses. I told them both that they were being silly to walk out of my class when it was clear to me that we were going to get along well.

Before the class was dismissed for lunch, I brought them back into our half-circle audience formation and presented the four students who had refused to participate.

The supportive teacher happened to walk in, as we were finishing our presentation, and realized that his wife shared my birthday. Small world! I love finding these connections through theatre exercises.

WHY AREN'T YOU RESPECTFUL?

My next class was the eighth grade. After doing our breathe-in and warm up game, we did an exercise on the value of silence and stillness. I briefly introduced their next lesson on active listening before it was time for dismissal. A few students left before I dismissed them. I caught them, running, in the hall, and reminded them that they needed to wait for me to dismiss them before leaving. As I let them go, I said, "Please walk respectfully in the hall, and down to lunch."

One of the students who had walked out the day before responded, "I am not respectful."

I asked him to stay back for a minute. "Let's talk about that," I said. "Why aren't you respectful?"

He replied, "My mom lets me do whatever I want."

"How's that working for you?" I asked. (I got this question from Dr. Phil.)

He went on to explain that he's been locked up several times. I knew some of this from the frustrated teacher who'd vented to me earlier in the week that this student had been on house arrest, and that he was going to "document him out" because,

140

"we don't need criminals in our schools." This means that my white male colleague, let's call him Mr. S., was going to try to write him up as much as possible so that, eventually, he'd be transferred to another school.

It often takes a book full of paperwork to prove that a disruptive student cannot properly function in a general education school, and may need an alternative environment. If you remember, earlier on, I said that my mother was once the director of Alternative Schools for Baltimore City. However, good teachers usually use this system of documentation to ensure that students who need more individual attention than a general education environment can provide will receive the services that they need. We don't usually write up incidents just because the student inconveniences us.

Examples of when this kind of consistent documentation is appropriate include a special-needs student who once threatened my colleague for an entire year, but was only transferred out of our school when he held a sign against my classroom window, stating, "Watch your daughter's back." My daughter was a second-grade student in the school where I taught at the time, and I almost lost my mind. After a complete breakdown, I told my administrators that only one of us could stay in the school. It would have to be him or me.

Another example was the student who had lead poisoning, resulting in brain damage, that once locked himself in a school closet, and ate crayons under a desk during my class observation. It took most of the year for me to convince the school, and his mom, that he needed an alternate setting. Once they finally agreed to move him to a self-contained classroom, they also decided that it would be a good idea to let him stay in my room for the rest of the week. I was surprised to see him the day after our meeting. It was that week that he picked a fight with a fifth-grader twice his size (he was in fourth grade) and was pummeled severely.

As a final example, I think of a student, we will call Akim, who gave me as much grief as the student with lead poisoning in the same fourth grade class. His mother is the one who told me, "At the beginning of the year, you looked like you were going to try to save the world. Now you look like you need a beer."

She also told me that she knew I couldn't handle her child, that it wasn't my fault, and that she had been trying to get him moved to "a Level Four" school. Instead of taking my word, or hers, the system sent "suits" to observe the class, and determined in their one-hour visit that Akim was perfectly capable of succeeding in a classroom with thirty other students.

In cases like these, we documented every occasion of crayon eating, fight picking and closet locking in the hopes of getting these students the special services they needed, while also protecting other students from their irrational behaviors.

So, anyway, this student, who we'll say goes by the nickname "Puff," proceeded to tell me that he behaves the way he does because he never gets any consequences. He talked about his probation officer, and how he was on "indefinite probation." Later I'd also learn that at fifteen, Puff already had a child, and allegedly he had another one on the way. He'd already told me in his interview the day before, that he'd like to be either a football player, or an engineer. Today, he relayed that he probably had a better chance of being an engineer because the chances of making it in the NFL are slim. I asked him about his grades and told him that he should go to the local high school that specializes in math, science and engineering.

He said his grades had fallen because, "I get depressed, and then I get angry, and then I act out." This statement strikes me as the most profound sentence in this entire memoir. If only we recognized and dealt with the cause of violence in young people — the depression of our youth — earlier in life, perhaps we could prevent the after-effects of anger and acting out. This solution would, of course, require as many layers as the problem itself. Mental health services and counseling are part of the answer, but we must also, as a society, address the multitude of societal issues that caused the depression in the first place. These include, but are not limited to, poverty, racism, mass incarceration, and, of course, the subject of this memoir — a broken, and dastardly designed, educational system.

In retrospect, I also think about my white, male colleague who told me he was "afraid I'm going to have to defend myself against them one day."

Puff had a friend, Keilan, who was also angry, and large for his age. One day, not long after our conversation, his friend tried to go after this same teacher because he was mad that the teacher had called his mom. I've since come to the realization that I may have saved his life that day, as I talked him down in the hallway, eventually got him to come back to my room, and spoke with him and Puff about the "school to prison pipeline."

"There are people who are waiting on you to mess up," I explained. "They have a cell ready, so they can exploit you for free labor. Don't fall into the trap."

Puff and his friend became leaders in my class after these interactions. They knew that I cared. They also knew that Mr. S was scared. In each instance, they behaved accordingly, wielding whatever power they had in whatever way they knew how.

I told Puff that I could relate to his anger issues, and that maybe he could use the breathing exercises we practiced in class to calm himself. I apologized, stating that "we" have failed him, and told him that he was welcome to come to my class to do his work, or take a break, as some other students did, when possible.

One of my former students stopped by and said, "I just wanted to give you a hug."

I interrupted our conversation to give her a hug, and he asked her if he could have a hug too.

She asked me if he deserved one, and I told her that he did, and that he'd been fine for me.

She hesitated, and he joked that he would hit her if she didn't hug him.

I reminded him that you can't force someone to hug you.
He went in for a hug anyway, squeezed her so tight that I could feel it. He had a football player's build. He didn't mean any harm, but he could easily cause some anyway.

I asked my female student if she was okay, and she assured me that she was fine.

I'd like to tell you that I explained to him why he needed to be gentle, and that he could easily serve as a much-needed protector, but I didn't have the energy that day. Instead, I let Puff go to lunch, and reflected on all of this after the fact.

DOES YOUR MOM PUNCH YOU WHEN SHE IS MAD?

One day I "pushed in" to my third grade class because it was raining, and they were housed in a separate building from the one where my classroom was located. The school expectation was that I would go to them, or "push-in" when there was inclement weather. Upon arriving in their classroom, two students were being pulled apart, by a few other students. They were trying to prevent a fight.

During the class, one of the students, we'll call him Quentin, spent the first half of the class glaring at his adversary. Several times he got up, and went close to the student, who seemed to have sparked his rage. Each time that he rose to fight, either myself, or one of the students in the room, removed him. I asked the feuding students if they wanted to talk about it. They both declined.

I tried to alleviate the situation by telling Quentin a funny story. When I asked if he wanted to hear a story, he shook his head no. I told him I was going to tell it to the class anyway. He covered his ears in defiance. He took his hands off of his ears when he saw how engaged the other students were with the story. It was about how I'd been involved in a conversation on Facebook about a "squeegee boy" who was accosted by the mayor because he wasn't in school. For those who aren't familiar, Baltimore squeegee boys stand on busy street corners with a squeegee and some cleaning agent, and offer to clean the car windows of passersby for change. According to the article I'd read, the mayor, while passing by, had yelled at this child to "go to school," and some friends and I were saying, on social media, that she should have taken more time to listen to him when he said, "I was going to, but…" We also felt that she could have used that opportunity to become involved in the young man's welfare.

Later, I'd learned that the mayor did follow up with the child. In the article stating this, I also learned that the mayor had started a "squeegee corps" where young men interested in entrepreneurship could learn about business and receive mentorship, while participating in group-fundraising efforts like car washes.

I was inspired by this story, and by a popular rap song with disturbing lyrics, to write a song with some of my seventh-graders about this squeegee corps to the tune of the rap, "Gucci Gang," that they were familiar with.

After sharing the tale with my third-graders, I played the song for them. They loved it!

Following the story and rap, and after going through our usual routine of breathing-in and doing a warmup, I asked the students to find a space in the room to work with their partners on their interviews.

I pulled Quentin, and another student, to the back of the room and asked Quentin's friend to explain to me what had happened.

He told me the student had pushed Quentin, and he had pushed him back.

I said, "Okay, he pushed you. You pushed him back. As far as I'm concerned, that should be the end of it, but you're letting him be the focus of your whole class. You can't even get your work done."

He said, "I want to punch him."

I asked "Does your mom punch you when she is mad?"

He replied, "Yes."

I wasn't prepared for that answer. I really wasn't. It hurt my heart.

I can't recall exactly what I said, there was a spirit speaking through me. It was something to the effect of, "I'm sorry. I'm really sorry that happened to you, and I'm sorry that you have learned that punching people is the only way to solve your problems. There really is another way, and I want you to learn it, because I want you to have a good life, and punching everyone who bothers you is not going to give you that."

Quentin started to cry. He cried for a while. I sent someone to get him tissue, and I held his hand while I interviewed his friend. Then I asked him if he was ready to work, and he said he was, so I interviewed him as well. He told me he was good at boxing, and that he had a boxing bag at home. I assured him that this could be a real career choice, and also was a great way to deal with his anger. I asked if he could let his anger go, so that we could return to the circle without him stalking the other child, and he said that he could. So he did.

When communicating with Facebook friends about the squeegee boy, I had made-up the name "Quentin" in order to humanize him. In the comments, I had joked, "If she'd talked to Quentin, she might have realized he was out there for a reason." I thought about my student Quentin on my drive home, and realized it was no mistake that his name had come to me before we met. I was supposed to help him. I shared what he said with his teacher, and vowed to share it with the school counselor the next day as well. This is my calling.

"STRONG" TEACHERS

Mid-to-late February is challenging for many teachers. We are far-enough removed from Christmas break, that we're starting to lose it, and yet, still so far from spring break that it doesn't feel close enough. One Tuesday in February, I had to call my agency to ask for a "mental health break" when Monday found me with not enough strength to get through another day. My first class was off, my second didn't care, and I had to evacuate my third class, when a student, who had kicked me the prior week, was back in class the next day, and started throwing chairs in my class. My fourth class, the one I'd been warned was the "worst in the school" was crazy as usual. I needed a day. I told my fifth and eighth-graders, the ones who were old enough to hear "the real," that I wasn't sure I'd be back at all. I called my program manager and said, "I need to take a mental health day, and if I don't see a change, I may need to put in my two weeks notice."

After dropping my daughter off at school on Tuesday, I came home and slept until noon. The night before, I'd received a message from one of my mentees, the one who started that poetry program I mentioned earlier, saying that she was in town and would like to see me. I told her I was taking the day off, and offered to do lunch at one. I was relieved when she hadn't responded, because I was still so tired. I watched the last few episodes of my latest Netflix obsession, "Being Mary Jane," until it was time to pick up my daughter from school.

My mentee finally responded to our messages from the prior night around five, saying that she'd been fighting with her family, but still wanted to see me. She admitted that she didn't have the funds to go anywhere. I was a day away from payday, and not able to sponsor dinner without a credit card, but offered to meet her at the gym that evening. I had a Planet Fitness Black card, which allowed guests in for free, at the rate of twenty dollars per month.

She seemed enthusiastic to meet me at the gym. We were supposed to meet at seven. I arrived a few minutes after seven, but there was no sign of my mentee yet. She called me at 7:30 to tell me that some friend and family drama was holding her up, but she was trying to get to me. One of my best friends called as I was waiting in the gym parking lot, which helped time fly by. Thank God, because it was almost an hour before she finally showed up.

My proposal was that we work out on three different cardio machines for 15 minutes each, to accommodate my A.D.D. She agreed, and the night staff was amicable to my request for both of us to use the hydromassage beds afforded by my Black Card. We both felt much better by the time we'd finished the session, having worked out our individual anxieties.

The next morning, I went to the gym again, this time with a friend. My program manager called me while I was there, to check in. I told her I had decided to try again, and I would let her know how it went.

I went back to work the next day. My third-graders asked me what I'd done the day before, and I admitted that I'd slept and watched TV. They were on their best behavior, as if they'd known the real reason for my absence.

My eighth-graders tried to be on their best behavior as well. One of the students, who'd walked out on me on Monday, after refusing my request for him to come sit next to me or take a behavior journal to my buddy room, said, "Miss Asia, are you okay? I'm good today."

Another student, who presented frequent challenges, said, "May I ask a question?"

"Sure," I responded.

"Why do you want to quit?" he asked.

I answered, honestly, "I am very sensitive, and this work is stressful, and is starting to depress me. If I was in my twenties, I could hang, but I'm almost forty. I'm getting tired."

He replied, "Thank you. I understand."

I went on to tell my students that I had asked for help. I explained that I was supposed to have an assistant, but she had disappeared.

One student called out, "I'll be your assistant."

Another replied, "And I'll be your assistant's assistant."

I laughed, thinking about an online educator's group I'm in, where I had recently replied to a post where someone said,

"I know I should leave, but I don't," with, "It's like an abusive relationship."

These are the moments that make us stay.

The next day I returned again, and responded to a quarrel between two of my students with, "Let me read you a story." Following up my attempt to mediate with asking one of the behavioral specialists to mediate between the boys, I read them the story <u>Desmond and the Very Mean Word</u> by Archbishop Tutu. One of the boys seemed mesmerized by the tale about empathy and forgiveness. He got it. The other seemed unaffected. Such is life.

My last class proved to me that they cared, as well.

We made it through our lesson, and I promised myself that we would try again tomorrow.

The next day, the assistant I hadn't seen in weeks met me in class. She told me that she had been assigned to another struggling school. Halfway through my first class, an additional support person appeared. She was a behavioral specialist sent by the agency I worked for.

At the beginning of my third class, the program manager showed up to observe. By now, with three guests, my class was on their best behavior, because, as I would later explain, "When they like you, they'll act right for company."

Because of this, however, they also made me look a little bit crazy, as if I had it all together all this time, and had the nerve to ask for help. I explained the theory about students putting on a show to my guests.

Despite the disruptive behaviors, it was clear that my students did really like me. Even the most frustrating students, if not especially them, thrive on the consistency of a caring teacher, as evidenced in my last class that day. The school-based behavior specialist escorted one of my most challenging students to my room. When the agency-based behavior specialist opened the door, he turned around screaming, "Oh, no!"

The school-based specialist said, "It's okay. She's here."

"I'm right here," I added, saying his name.

"Oh, alright," he said, turning back around, entering the room, and finding a spot next to me, as had become his habit.

That night, I also received a call from an additional person from my agency asking me to detail my concerns. At that moment, I was sure they were taking me seriously. I remembered the words of the behavioral specialist who visited that day, "They really don't want to lose strong teachers." This is what it feels like to be supported.

The moral of this story is that even strong teachers have to remember to ask for help.

The following is a list of Facebook posts I've decided to include about teaching. I often use the social media tool as a way to engage my community in conversations about education. It's also a helpful tool to share best practices and to commiserate with colleagues.

THIS IS HOW THEY GET YA

March 13, 2018

In today's episode of "This is how they get ya" (and because I didn't get to work on my books this weekend). My principal comes to observe my last class today, the one that I mentioned before I had been warned is the worst in the school. I am eating Cheetos (because my 20 minute break turned into a five minute break, when the teacher was seven minutes late picking up her class due to a meeting, and because I had to call a parent) and playing music like I usually do during the first five minutes of class. After the five minutes, I try to settle the class down to no avail. One student, in particular, (who I was told had transferred yesterday, but lo and behold, is back again today) is wildin'! I go through my behavior management system: warning, sit next to me, sit in the in-class reflection area, take the behavior journal to my buddy room — but he refuses to leave the room.

The principal asks if he needs to see the counselor, and suggests that I ignore him. I'm thinking, "Get this Gremlin out of my room!"

She tells him he may not get "resource" anymore if he continues to behave this way. He gets smart with her again, and I say, in my Mama voice, "Who are you talking to?"

Again, she suggests I ignore him, and asks him to talk in the hall. He refuses to leave, again, but somehow, someway, she convinces him to join my class circle.

Meanwhile I mentioned to the class that I'd received an email from my admin today about them leaving the building before I dismiss them. "While the principal is here," I say, "raise your hands if you were here the several times we had this conversation. Raise your hand if you were here for the line drill. Raise your hand if I called your parents last week for this same issue. You are embarrassing me!"

After our breathe-in and warm-up game, I begin my lesson on objectives and tactics. I share my personal objective for the class, give another example by reviewing the Big Bad Wolf's objective in "The Three Little Pigs," and, then ask my students to raise their hands to share their personal objectives. The most challenging student shares that he'd like to be a professional ball player. I go around to the rest of my students, and am preparing to move into tactics, when he says, "I have another one." I make the decision to humor him.

He says, "If I can't be a ball player, I want to be a doctor who works on cancer patients. My best friend died of cancer when I was young, and that's when I started acting bad."

I remind my class of the story we read the day before about why people behave the way they do. I ask my student the name of his friend, and request a moment of silence for him. I then go and hug this student, and stand behind him, with my hand on his shoulder for the next five minutes.

157

We review tactics, but as we do, one student shouts out that another student just called yet another challenging student a "b%$&*." I tell him that everything's not worth repeating, and we shouldn't spread "mess." I go on to share how one student's father had shared, the week before, that he sometimes worries that his son might be the next school shooter due to all of the bullies in my class.

I say, "I know a lot of us have anger issues, self included."

The first challenging student stands up, "I know I do."

"Many of us are on the edge, and can be pushed over, at any moment," I continue. I go on to tell them about being bullied in middle school, and the time I was jumped (they say banked) every day for a week, and how I eventually blacked out, and attacked the instigator. "By the time I finally fought back, I was so angry I could have killed that girl."

One student calls out that he would have brought a gun.

I tell him we aren't even going to speak like that.

I relay that every choice we make affects others. I have a daughter who needs me alive, and every student in this class also has people who love and need them.

The original challenger says his mom is not around. I say, "That is not okay, but you still have people who love you. I love you."

As we line up to leave, following the announcements, the student who flipped out last week, says, "It's in the school pledge. Each choice I make affects me and others." I agree.

The student who called him a "B" approaches him, and apologizes. He says, "I accept your apology, but please don't do it again. I could have flipped out, and you know how I get when I flip."

Yet another student approaches me to tell me how she snapped on one of her classmates earlier today. I hold her hand, and listen to her story, as I lead my class out of the school.

Perhaps the moral of my story is: *listening, and love, saves lives.*

March 15, 2018
My babies did such a brilliant job on their assignment this week. It gave me life! The work was on objectives, tactics, obstacles and motivation — which we've been discussing all week. Even the eighth-grader who never does any written work turned in *something*! Let me tell you — these students have dreams and plans, including college, careers, and entrepreneurship. They are clear about the obstacles they'll face along the way, but they have motivation strong enough to overcome them. One thing that struck me, today, was how many students are motivated by either giving back to their parents, or families, or inspiration they've received from people they're paying attention to. I'm out of bulletin board space, so I hope to create a board that doesn't yet exist in the halls next week. They deserve to be celebrated, and their work should be shared!

March 19, 2018

Today was a pretty good day. First off, shout out to Mother Nature for the brief reprieve before the predicted snow.

Second, I tried to call a parent today about a student who was out of order several times last week, and acting up again today. I meant to call last week, but got busy, so today I stopped my class to make the call. The phone was turned off. I verify with my student that the phone is off, and ask him how he gets home. He tells me he walks. "Okay, I'll be walking you home today," I say.

When the general education teacher shows up, I inform her of my plan "in case he tries to duck me." Lo and behold, his mom AND dad show up in my room two hours later. They say they frequently pop up on him in school, and will be happy to pop into my class too. Mom says she needs to pay her phone bill, but asks for MY number. Dad asks what he did that was so bad that I was going to walk him home. I say, "He wasn't THAT bad. He's not throwing chairs or anything, but he is consistently disruptive."

I offer a few examples: bothering other students, especially putting his hands on them, calling out, etc. "He's very smart though," I tell them. I give them two of his behavior journals so they can read his explanations for his behavior.

"I like you," Dad says, and they leave with the promise to check in. Yay parents!!

Third, my most challenging class was missing some students, and they actually got to do some work today. I tell them if they finish the first part of their assignment, they can play a second round of mum ball. The assignment is about conflict, and most of them are eager to share their work.

As they're playing their second game, the "ref" apparently makes a bad call, and another student calls a time-out to explain. I say "Okay, but in the future, you have to respect the ref." Another student, who is very bright, but behaviorally challenged says, "The ref is only there to resolve conflict."

"I love you..." I say, calling his name.

"I may be angry, but I'm also a peacekeeper," he says.

Day made!

March 23, 2018
So not only did the parents I posted about on Monday stop by, as promised, but mom asked what we were learning about, and took over my girls' group after I told her. Dad pulled the boys over for a chat in the meantime. This is what parental involvement looks like!

March 29, 2018
Today I wanted to dedicate, at least, a short chapter to my student Keilan. I mentioned Keilan before in this writing, when I described two students who walked out of my class the second week of the third quarter, when I asked them to interview each other and present their findings.

Keilan is also the one who walked out of my class again after refusing to take a behavior journal to my buddy room when he had exhausted all other consequences. He refused, and left without the journal. This was only one of many reasons I threatened to quit that day. I left his class with a speech about how anyone with options wouldn't be insane enough to stay in that school, in that situation, and a plea that those who were serious about their future, read and study outside of school.

However, when I returned, Keilan was the one who said, "Miss Asia, you okay? I'm good today." From that point on, whenever I am visibly frustrated in class, Keilan says, "Miss Asia, I got you," and will bring the class to order.

The quarter lasts ten weeks, and it may have been week seven, when Keilan hugged me upon arrival in my class on a Friday. While sitting between him and "Puff," as had become my custom, I noticed the strong scent of marijuana. I joked with both students that someone smelled "ripe." James pointed to Keilan. Keilan denied the claim, but spent the rest of my class in a bit of a stupor. This was, actually, out of character for him, as he was usually quite animated.

Sitting next to them both, I texted a friend that I might have been developing a "contact high," particularly because I was unusually amused by the newest emojis on my Android.

At one point, Keilan exited the room without permission for a few minutes. Upon his return, I reminded him that he needed to ask to leave the room in the future. I reiterated that since I am responsible for my students during that time, it is imperative that I know their whereabouts, particularly in the event of a drill or emergency.

A few minutes later, one of the part-time counselors I don't see at school very often entered the room, searching for a student. She asked what grade I had, and when I told her eighth, she relayed that she had the wrong room.

Keilan, asked me, a few minutes before class was over, who the counselor had asked for.

"She said she had the wrong room," I relayed. "Why, did you think she was looking for you?"

Paranoia? I wondered.

He told me that he wasn't sure, and that she had come to visit him at home, once before, because his mom had asked her to.

"I think she thought she could help me," he admitted, "but we just played Uno."

I wondered what kind of trauma Keilan might have faced that prompted his mom's request.

"So, you thought I was high?" he continued. "I don't even smoke."

"That's good," I responded, "but, yes, I think you could use some oil," I joked.

The following Monday I brought Keilan some essential oil, patchouli, from an essential oil kit I had at home.

He refused to accept my offering, stating, "I'll just use Axe," but another student asked me to leave the oil with him.

Fast-forward to our eighth week, and Keilan has seemed himself since. He still offers to bring the class to order, whenever I seem flustered.

At some point, I ask him where Puff is, because I haven't seen his friend at school all week.

He tells me he doesn't know.

"You guys don't call or text?" I query.

"My phone is broken," he replies.

"And you don't live close to each other?" I continue.

"Not anymore," he says.

"Actually," he goes on, "I did see him outside once, but he was smoking, and I'm not trying to do that anymore."

"Anymore?" I laugh.

"I mean, I never did," he replies, laughing back.

"So, how are your grades?" I ask.

"I mean, they're good. I'm passing."

"Passing doesn't mean good," I remind him.

"Well, I have a B in language arts and social studies," he says.

"B. As in…?" I say.

"B, as in Boy," he laughs. "I just need to get my grade up in math."

"I can help you with that," says his new friend, the student who just transferred in after being expelled from a local boarding school for cursing out a teacher.

I wipe the tears developing in my eyes. One of my pet pleasures in life is seeing students (actually anyone) support each other.

"That's beautiful," I say, sincerely.

April 17, 2018
Upon Reflection…

Sometimes the answers come to me in song lyrics. Yesterday was the start of a new quarter, and let me tell you, it was a doozy.

I only had my first class for twenty minutes because both of the grade-level teachers were out, and both classes were outside, but no one told me to pick them up.

My second class is a repeat of one of my most challenging classes from the first quarter. They're baaack!

My third class has 31 students, including 8 students from the "Life Skills" class. At least it comes with 3 assistant teachers!

My fourth class, though. Lawd, my fourth class — was *off the chain*! I tried "managing" them to no avail, when one of them announced, "We are the worst class in the school. Some people, you just can't change."

I tried stopping the class to call a parent, but the number was busy. The student had given me the number, so I used my class roster to find out if he was telling the truth. I called the listed number, and mom told me she was "on the way." Unfortunately, I realized minutes later, that I had accidentally called the parent of another student, in the same grade, with the same name, who is never a problem. Another student refused to tell me his name, when I tried to call his parents. I, in turn, refused to let the class leave until he did. We waited ten minutes for anyone to tell me. Eventually, I gave up and let them go.

Upon reflection, however, I realized I hadn't handled it well. My classroom is not big enough for me, my students, and my ego. I let my ego get the best of me yesterday.

I can't remember if it was last night, or this morning. They tend to blend together sometimes, when the line from "Frozen" came to me, "People make bad choices if they're mad or scared or stressed. But throw a little love their way and you'll bring out their best."

I realized I had been responding from a place of stress yesterday, and they were probably coming from a place of anger, but I could choose love today.

I started my thirteen-hour day in the gym, accompanied by my friend Ra, who threw a little love my way. Rasheem is one of those people who's good for your self-esteem: open, accepting, complimentary — you know the type. After some time, and talking, on the treadmill with my homegirl, I got my hydro-massage while listening to binary beats, high frequency meditation music.

I was in a much better place to receive my students today. I was running late, but I cued up Drake's song "God's Plan" as I approached my school, preparing for my first class. Most of my students love this song, and we enjoy singing the catchy part, together, where he sings, "She asked do you love me, I said only partly. I only love my bed, and my mama, I'm sorry."

Fast forward to my last class, and the two students I had so much trouble with yesterday showed up early. I'd told them both that until I spoke with a parent of the first student, and got the name of the second student, they could not return to my class. I reiterated my statement upon their arrival, and they asked if they could enter if the first student promised to be good, and the second told me his name. I acquiesced. The first student still gave me some trouble, but not nearly as much as yesterday. Because I am not beholden to a pacing guide, like so many teachers less fortunate than myself, I simply stopped the class each time he interrupted.

At one point, I asked the class, "So you've been dealing with this all year? I'm sorry."

Another student responded, with exasperation, "Yes. Thank you!" I heard in his tone, "Thank you for acknowledging that this is frustrating for ALL of us."

We didn't make it to our game, but at some point, I allowed the students to vote on whether they wanted to continue trying to get through our breathing exercises, which kept being interrupted, so we could play the game I planned, or stop and try again tomorrow. The challenging student voted to try again, but he was outvoted by his classmates. Then the afternoon announcements came on. We'll try again tomorrow.

If you've read this far, I thank you for caring, and I'll reward you for your efforts with the kicker.

When I looked up the lyrics to the Frozen song, which is called "Fixer Upper," the lines before the ones I quoted read, "We're not saying you can change him/Cause people don't really change/ We're only saying that love's a force/that's powerful and strange."

Just. Wow!

MORE ABOUT CLASS SIZE
BECAUSE I CAN NOT SAY ENOUGH ABOUT IT'S IMPORTANCE

May 24, 2018

I had fourteen students in my seventh grade class today, which is how it should be, in my opinion. At one point, I gave a student, who alternates between my general education and special education population, a direction. It took him a minute to oblige, and my general education students started yelling at him, because they know how I get when they don't follow directions the first time. This time, however, I asked them to stop yelling, and relayed that the student sometimes needs a minute or two, to process my directions, but will usually follow them after. Sometimes I need to repeat them. I went on to share how my own A.D.D. results in processing issues that sometimes make people think I'm being rude. "Sometimes it takes a minute for things to make their way from one side of my brain to the other."

I further admitted that I sometimes have to repeat very simple requests from my students, particularly after a taxing day like: "Can-you-go-to-the-bathroom? Yes."

As a result of my own admission, I noticed a couple students sharing their own processing issues with each other, with no shame. One student was comparing his "issues" to the

Transformers cartoon. I think it's so important that we share our own imperfections with the students we serve, so that they begin to realize that we all have strengths and weaknesses, but this doesn't have to mean that we're completely dysfunctional. It only means that we recognize that *most* of us need accommodations, of some sort. It is essential that we learn to accommodate ourselves, accordingly.

May 27, 2018
It makes me both depressed and angry when I think about how much of my created curriculum my current set of students didn't get to. There were so many exercises and activities we didn't implement, so many lessons that went half, or untaught, due to factors including class size and dynamic, behavior management, burnout and exhaustion. I've mentioned these elements in a previous chapter, but they warrant repeating here.

My first class has been labeled one of the most challenging students in an already difficult school. This class includes several students with "504" plans, which mitigate students' behavioral challenges by providing individualized classroom accommodations. The proposed strategies for two of these students include allowing them breaks on their iPads.

As you might imagine, this particular strategy poses a significant distraction to the rest of the class. There are one to two fights per day, in my class alone, with this group of students, on average. I have a few students who walk in and out of my room, at will, to the point where, lately I've just started locking my doors when they leave, so that I can focus on the other students. This may, or may not, be the best strategy for dealing with these behaviors, but it is overwhelming, and I'm at my wits' end.

There was, however, one day, when some students were testing and others were absent, that I ended up with sixteen students in this class. At dismissal, their classroom teacher inquired about their behavior, and I responded, "There were sixteen students today. It was dreamy."

The teacher replied that she feels like sixteen should be the maximum for a Title I school (for those who aren't familiar, Title I means most students are eligible for free or reduced lunch, meaning they are living in poverty). I told the teacher she should run for president, and she relayed that she really does want to go into policy. I hope she does. We need more people who are intimately familiar with our challenges to go into government. One, particularly bright, student, over-hearing our conversation, said that she wants to run for president. I truly hope she has that opportunity as well.

My second class is, in my opinion, the most challenging of grades: seventh. They are the only class I have had twice this year, due to a scheduling issue. They also come with five or six students from a self-contained special education class, whose social skill goals are met with inclusion in my "resource" class. Because this is their second quarter with me, I have been tasked with creating an entirely separate curriculum for them. In some ways, it is easier this quarter because they are already familiar with my rules, routines, and procedures. The teacher of the general education class is particularly supportive, as well, but both of my teary breakdowns this year happened after this class. One was in the first quarter, and another this quarter.

My third class of first-graders is manageable, by itself, but they are joined with another ten students from the "Life Skills" class. Fortunately, one of the general education first-graders, and one of the Life Skills students have "one-on-one" assistants, who are there to support only them, but who will also assist with tasks like classroom management and copying.

Still, while one of these assistants was busy with her charge this week, the other came into my room, curled up on the pillows in my library, and went to sleep. I actually don't blame her. It was a Thursday, at the end of the year, and we were all at the end of our rope, and coping as best we could.

My fourth class of fifth-graders were the ones who warned me, week one, that they were "the worst class in the school." There are a few volatile personalities, resulting in a lot of insults, and disruptive behavior. One student, in particular, decides, on a daily basis, whether we will work or not. If he decides we aren't, he will monopolize my entire class, by doing things like opening the window and cursing at people outside, insulting students, picking fights, and flat out refusing to follow any directions I give.

The way our behavior management system is set up, I can ask him to leave class to fill out a behavior journal after I have reminded him of the class expectations, ask him to sit next to me, and ask him to sit in the class reflection area. However, there is no recourse in place after he returns with the completed journal and continues to act out, other than to call home, or write an office referral. I have done both. I have called his grandmother, because I was told she is a more effective disciplinarian than his mom, which I definitely believe, particularly given that he returned from a ten-day suspension with fresh Jordans on his feet. I was vexed! Still, there was little to no improvement, even after the call. It is exhausting!

With three and a half weeks left in the school year, my seventh grade special education students were moved to another resource class, and my fifth grade "monopolizer" earned himself a thirty-day suspension, meaning he will be out for the rest of the year.

I'm not going to lie. I'm ecstatic about that first part, and both sad, and glad, about the latter. I created a project on the Baltimore Ceasefire initiative for my seventh-graders in the first part of the quarter, but I've been a little lost on where to go with them since. They've had quite a few free-days.

Now, I'm working with a local agency that is responsible for seeking community input about their neighborhood, as their school is being rebuilt next year. Having a few less students in my class will make this project so much more feasible.

As for my suspended student, I like him. I love him. He is a leader and he is very smart. I pray it's not too late for him to receive the intensive intervention he is going to need to recover from the death of his brother last year, and whatever else he has going on. On the other hand, I was able to teach my class on Friday, and I was happy for the other students who've suffered so long, due to his inability to function in my class. I've been told that because I have them at the end of the day, is why he was so out of control in mine.

Regardless, his severe consequence also seems to have mellowed a couple of other challenging students, including his sidekick, who was eerily quiet on Friday. Of course, the sidekick's mom had also visited my class on Friday, where she found him, lying on the floor, being attacked by a female student he'd insulted one too many times. She told me that my class was out of control, and all I could do was agree, in all humility.

I'd like to tell you that I was embarrassed, but I'd moved beyond embarrassed at this point. The phrase I kept finding myself using was "over it."

LAYERS OF EDUCATION

It's been a challenge to keep telling this story. I've found myself growing bitter, after so many years in education. I mean, it couldn't possibly remain this way, if people actually *cared!* There have been days I have shared excerpts from my experience on social media to absolutely no response. However, there have been other days when I have shared, and received many responses. There have also been calls and messages from friends encouraging me to keep going.

This impetus to write was sparked by a question posed by a stranger in one of my educator's groups, and his response to my replies, which reminded me that there are some who are interested in my experience, and since I have so much to say, and I find this cathartic, regardless of readership, I will continue.

I have recently identified a few layers to our education problem in America. I will attempt to dissect them henceforth.

At the top layer, we have a system that is not designed for the general populace, and particularly low-income black and brown children, to succeed. This system works best when most people remain poorly educated, appeased by the few modern comforts they are afforded, and, eventually, forced to work for the one to three percent of rich, white men who run this nation. To those in power, this system is running perfectly fine according to it's design, and while it makes me bitter, it is important for me to remember. They don't care about *us*, at all.

On the second layer, we have well meaning policy makers who are so disconnected from the realities of our schools, that they make poor decisions, based on their own experiences, that have little to nothing to do with the actual needs of the populations I serve. They probably care, they just don't get it — at all!

While sharing my theory with a friend, she wisely noted that those on this second tier don't really care either, for if they did, they'd do their due diligence to understand the needs, and realities, of our public school students and teachers. Fair enough.

On the third layer, we have administrators and policy makers who, sometimes blindly, follow the mandates of the first two tiers, even when it is clear to anyone with common sense, and critical thinking skills, that these policies make little, or no sense. They say things like "rules are rules" and "laws are laws," as if they have no sense of history. They believe slavery is in the distant past, and racism was an inconvenience eradicated by Martin Luther King.

Many of them care about our children. More care, however, about their mortgages, and affording the private school tuitions of their own "special" offspring. A great deal of these "middle" men and women have convinced themselves that the parents are the problem, and that these kids are holding themselves back. Every once in a while they may quote a book about "systemic racism," and claim they are fighting against it, but as long as they can pay into their 401k, take a few vacations, and gas up their luxury cars, they'll soon go along with whatever latest program those in tiers one and two are pushing at the moment.

Meanwhile, program creators in those first and second layers are getting rich off of the creation of the latest trendy programs, tests and curriculums, adopted by those in the third layer, at the expense of our children.

Then, I guess, we have to admit there is a fourth layer. It would include teachers, and administrators, like myself, who are frustrated by all of the above, but remain poor and powerless because we've refused to play a game we clearly see was never meant for us to win. Maybe we write a book, and pontificate with like-minded intellectuals over coffee and cocktails. Maybe we start an organization or try to take over organizations, like teachers' unions that might make a difference. Maybe we just keep showing up in our schools, and our classrooms, teaching as best as we can, and praying that one day, one of our students might heed the call, and become the change we've been praying for. Maybe we have children, and teach them everything we know, with the hope that they can create another way. Maybe we homeschool. Maybe we start programs and schools. Maybe we run for political office.

At this point in my own journey, I just want to finish sharing what I've learned and expatriate, at least for a while, as I recover from the post-traumatic-stress-disorder of an overachiever who's been set up to fail, time and time again. I still "Teach like a Champion," but I no longer expect to win.

TOO MANY HOLES

I came up with an analogy to explain teacher burnout that I've shared with a couple of colleagues who immediately understood. If you've ever read, or heard of the story, "I'm a Bucket Filler," you will easily comprehend my comparison. If not, no worries. I will attempt to explain. Please picture that I, and any other good teacher, am a vessel. Imagine any large cup, bowl or jar. Each weekend I fill myself up with reading, writing, exercise, prayer/meditation, and time with family and friends who share my values of peace, love and joy.

Every Monday, however, I am met at the door with students who come with the straws of poverty, abandonment, and neglect. "Can I sit next to you?" "Can you tell so-and-so to stop calling me names?" "What are we doing today?" "I don't want to do that." Et cetera, et cetera. My vessel is quickly emptied, and only filled by students, colleagues and administration who thank me for my work, catch onto concepts quickly, or repeat something I said, or did, in a prior lesson, reminding me that they are paying attention, and my work is not in vain. It is rare that they are able to fill as fast as they drain, through no real fault of their own. There are simply too many holes.

LEARNING THROUGH FAILURE

There is so much I could, and want to say, around this topic. Most of all, I'd like to relay how astounded I have been by how little our students understand about the purpose of failure. Whenever I've had adults come to visit my class, I've been pleasantly surprised by their willingness to participate, but dismayed by their general propensity to provide answers and solutions before allowing my children to struggle, even a little.

One of my favorite tests, as a full-time teacher, was giving my students a quiz, the first week of school, the answers to which were posted around the room. It was always amazing to see how many youth would give up on themselves before even trying. Lesson one, I'd later explain, is that, "Sometimes the answers are right in front of you." One of our classroom Big Goals was "Learn to Use your Resources." This is a life skill.

Still, even when the answers are not provided, I'm a huge proponent of failure. I believe we retain information best when we struggle to obtain it.

My sister can tell you how upset I was when she provided my daughter with a hint I felt was too huge, for a game (Fuzzy Wuzzy) I played with my daughter for almost a year. I played the same game, one I learned in college, with my middle school students for months, usually during any kind of transition, and never gave them the answer. The success they felt once they figured it out for themselves was, in my opinion, worth all of the strife.

In my teacher training, I learned to allow students at least fifteen seconds of think-time before calling on someone else, once I've asked them for an answer. This type of pause, and patience, has been instrumental in my instruction.

Even in my warm-up name games, I ask my students to give their peers ten seconds of think-time before offering suggestions, and then only if the student has asked for help. Another BIG Class Goal of mine is "Learn when to ask for help." This is another life skill.

As I've made my tour of Baltimore City Schools, I have learned over and over again how averse our students are to failure. I have made it a personal mission to instill in them the knowledge that mistakes are a tool for growth.

Anyone who knows me can tell you what a huge proponent I am of project-based learning. I have yet to see a tool as effective for learning as trying, getting it wrong, and trying again. As I complete this fifth, and final round of edits on the book you are reading, I offer it as evidence.

In my second year of teaching, I argued with an administrator who admonished me for not using the standard protocol of "I do, We do, You do." In this mode of instruction, you model the task, then do the task together, then allow students to try the task on their own. I told my admin that some of my students were so arrogant, I had to let them start with the "You do," then show them where they got it wrong. Many of them truly believe they already know everything, but then again, so do a lot of adults. I once read somewhere that Americans were number one in confidence, but around, number twenty-two in actual education.

I believe that we must learn to cherish the process of learning, trying, failing, and trying again, and again, in order to learn our lessons best. As someone who has failed a lot, I speak from experience!

THREE MONTHS IN A MONTESSORI

The following section, as we near the end of my narrative, has been the most difficult to write. It is perhaps, the most painful, and certainly, the most revised. It's been challenging to convey the series of unfortunate events that led to one of my most humbling educational experiences. Those events included my personal failure to negotiate a contract that would protect me, an unusually hot fall in a school with only partial air conditioning, a series of problematic interactions with stores and restaurants in an underserved community that left me "hangry," an inopportune interaction with a class and teacher, on my most emotional day of the month, and more.

As I have detailed in other chapters, my time at the Title I school where I taught in South Baltimore was particularly challenging, but I managed to make it through the year with the support of an incredible team.

The principal asked me to return in April. She stated that she didn't have the budget to hire me through my agency, but if I had my degree, she was willing to use her arts budget, allocated by the city, to fund my position. I told her I'd think about it, but that my inclination was to decline. In May, she relayed that she'd located the funding to hire me back through the agency if I so desired. I told her the truth, that I was tired, and politely declined.

I then relayed to my agency's hiring director that I'd like to continue with the agency, but that I needed either an easier assignment, or at least one that was closer. I'd been commuting thirty minutes each way for the prior two years.

A few weeks later, my director reported back that the former vice-principal of my last school was willing to hire me at her new school. I investigated the reviews, and found that it was still poor-performing, and it was only a few minutes closer than my former drive.

"Let's hold out, and see if we can do better," I said.

Two weeks later I received a message from a Facebook friend stating that her school was looking for a part-time arts instructor.

The hours the school was interested in were not enough to fulfill my financial needs, and I told her so, but sent my résumé, anyway, at her request.

She asked me to send a sample lesson plan, and I did that as well, again stating that I needed a particular amount of hours to survive, but suggesting that we keep each other updated on our hiring, and interviewing, process. Her principal, then, reached out to me to schedule an interview.

I brought the portfolio my previous agency had required us to create. The principal loved my curriculum, and vowed to do her best to create a schedule that would suit both of our needs. I asked to see the potential space, and she obliged, also offering a tour of the school, which included a small kitchen where students could learn culinary arts. There was also a chicken coop on the grounds, and a small garden. I was impressed by the leader and the facilities, and told her I would need at least twenty hours of consistent work at twenty-five dollars an hour to commit to their program.

I shared, "At this point, with my daughter entering high school, I just want to pay my bills."

Some of you are probably wondering, now, how I managed to pull off these minimal working hours. I've lived with my mother, who retired a few years prior to this writing, since I left grad school. I've paid towards rent and utilities with my tax refund each year, but not nearly enough to compensate for all that she's given me. However, we've always believed that if I stick to my path, I'll be able to pay her back, eventually.

Anyways, the principal sent me a series of emails, stating that she was still very interested in hiring me, and was working on a schedule. Once class days and times were finalized, she sent a final memorandum of understanding (M.O.U.), offering me my proposed twenty hours at twenty-five dollars an hour. I was thrilled! The philosophy of the school, which emphasized the joy of learning, seemed very much in line with my personal philosophy of ensuring that my students develop a love of learning.

When my summer program ended early that August, I asked if I might drop my materials off to save myself the trouble of moving everything back home, and then back to another school. The principal agreed.

A week before school began, I set up the space, asking my mother to sew fabrics that could cover outdated blackboards, bulletin boards and whiteboards that were no longer usable (some had been written over with permanent marker, thus making them impossible to clean.) Next I mapped out the room, and created centers, deciding to use an awkward wooden frame, leftover from some long-forgotten production, as a library cubby. Then, devoting different corners of the room for art, costume, game and puppet centers. I hadn't negotiated time for set-up in my contract, but listed the seven and a half hours it took on my timesheet, with hopes they'd compensate me in good faith.

I was compensated for my set-up time, but there was a financial dilemma the first week of school. I had budgeted for being off work the month between summer camp and the first week of school, but hadn't foreseen that the city would declare half-days for all schools without air conditioning. When that encompassed the first four days of school, I was left in a financial bind. I hadn't considered including these possibilities in my contract.

Only the middle school at my new placement had air, and this was just my first class of the day. Without the elementary classes, I would lose out on about $400 of anticipated income that first week. At first, I was fine with missing a day or two. It gave me a chance to observe the other classes, which a colleague had suggested I do anyway. By day three, however, I began to feel anxious. I spent my free-time, mostly, in the air-conditioned middle and upper schools, as the heat was truly unbearable on the lower levels. I observed one of the teachers there, and bonded with her and one of the assistants, who was also new to the school.

185

It was the assistant, who suggested on the third day that I conduct a theatre workshop with the middle school that might earn me an extra hour or two, while one of the teachers was in a meeting. The teacher thought this was a great idea. Unfortunately, another of the upper school teachers had lost his mother prior to the start of the school year, and was out, as a result. The decision had been made to keep two of the middle school classes together, which left me with one class of thirty-five instead of two classes of seventeen or eighteen.

The day that it was suggested I conduct a workshop, I had only brought a plum for a snack, believing that I'd be back home within an hour or two. When the extra class was suggested, I relayed that I would go and grab lunch, and come back before the teacher's meeting.

On my way out, I asked another colleague where teachers generally got food in the area. She said that most went to Starbucks. I put Starbucks in my GPS, and noted that it was a seven-minute walk. A fourteen-minute round-trip walk in the kind of heat that shut schools down was not at all appealing. The school had turned most of the faculty parking into a playground for the youth, and the bit of parking that remained was for full-time teachers to share, so my car was parked a few minutes walk away. I looked around, and noticed a corner store just a couple of blocks away, not far from where I'd parked my car, and decided to grab a snack there instead. Once inside, a sign informed me that they didn't accept credit cards. I didn't have any cash on me, but saw that there was another corner store a block away, right near where I'd parked. I walked there, only to be informed that they, too, had a "cash only" policy.

"Okay," I thought to myself, "I'm very close to my car now, and I have about twenty minutes before I need to be back. There must be a McDonald's close. If I drive there, and grab a bite, I can park my car back at the school, since some teachers are bound to have left, given the early dismissal."

I jumped in my car, and navigated to a McDonald's. Sure enough, there was one just three minutes away. I arrived and placed my order within another three minutes, but the line was moving super slow. One woman behind me called out of her window, after a few minutes of waiting, "This is crazy, ain't it?"

"It's ridiculous," I responded.

Finally, I got to the window, and the cashier asked me if I'd ordered a Big Mac. I had not. I told her so. She asked me about another wrong order, and I informed her that I'd ordered a Filet-O-Fish meal. She began typing something into her computer.

At this point, I had ten minutes remaining before I needed to be back for my workshop.

"Are you just now placing the order?" I asked incredulously.

"Yes," she responded sheepishly.

"Never mind," I said, and drove off.

I was, probably, then, a bit "hangry" when I conducted my middle school workshop that day, but I tried not to take it out on the students. I led them through my rap of rules, my breathe-in procedure, and a warm-up game before closing with a brief reflection activity.

Two days later, during my usually scheduled time with that class, their teacher asked if I'd mind meeting them in her room, instead of mine, as the other teacher had yet to return, and they were still together as a group of thirty-five. I agreed to do so, but promised myself that we'd simply review the rules and breathe-in, and play another warm-up game, and then I'd take them outside, so as not to overwhelm them, or myself, by trying to navigate such a large group.

This time, however, the students were out of control. They wouldn't even close their eyes for the breathe-in activity, and several of them just stared at me. I pointed this out, and tried to start over, but a few continued staring at me, and others started chatting with each other, even though I'd emphasized that this was the "silent and still" section of our class, and being silent and still was my number one lesson in theatre.

After the third time of trying to start over with the breathe-in, to no avail, I stopped and asked the students to do a written reflection, stating what had happened during this time.

"If you were doing what you were supposed to do," I said, "just write what you witnessed."

Some students refused to write anything, while others, mostly the students who hadn't given me any problems, began handing in their reflections. I started reading them to myself. One student had written, "It's strange how the students who needed to breathe the most refused to do it."

I read her sentiments aloud, and said that I agreed. When the teacher finally returned, I shared my disappointment with how the class had gone.

I checked in with her, at the end of the day, and she relayed that the students thought I was "mean," and had gone overboard in my handling of the situation. I reiterated that they were really rude, and agreed to try again the following week.

When those students came the next week, it was evident that they had decided they didn't like me, and didn't have to do what I asked them to do. Adding insult to injury, I just happened to be on the second day of my cycle, a day I often joke, that I shouldn't even have to leave the house.

When the teacher, Miss Karen, came to retrieve her class, I was almost in tears.

"I'm not sure I'm going to be able to do this," I shared.

The next day the principal asked to meet me after school.

She started off by sharing that the lower school students really seemed to enjoy my class. Then, she went on to share that the upper school felt I was disrespectful.

"I feel disrespected," I retorted.

"But we are the adults," she replied.

I tried to explain that I felt betrayed by the teacher having gone to her so quickly. She told me that Miss Karen had relayed that she tried to talk to me once. She went on to share that the assistant I thought I'd bonded with indicated that she also felt that I was out of order in my previous class. I was saddened by this, and said, "I thought she was my friend, but I guess I won't have friends." In retrospect, I realize this was an emotional and egotistical response.

I told the principal that I was a big believer in direct communication. She suggested that we schedule another meeting with the teacher-in-question, to see if the situation could be resolved. The meeting was scheduled for the following Monday.

In the next week's meeting, the principal relayed some of my points from the following meeting back to me, saying that she was just trying to communicate directly, per my stated preference, before the arrival of the teacher. The teacher, upon entering, shared that she felt my program was salvageable if I was willing to work with the students. I agreed to try, despite having written an unsent email over the weekend, stating that I didn't believe I could work with the students if I wasn't going to be supported. I did ask if the students might receive grades for my class, as they'd indicated, previously, that they wouldn't take my class seriously otherwise. The principal acquiesced to my request, particularly after I promised to frame it as, "You guys won." "That's great," she said.

The week before I had asked the staff member in charge of supplies if I could have some chart paper. She said she wasn't sure she had any, but the vice principal shared that she had some in her office that she could lend out. I took the chart paper from the V.P.'s office before the supply controller relayed that she'd found a pad she could give me. I put the vice principal's paper back in her room, and stored the new pad in mine.

A day or two later, the vice principal, Miss Vee, asked if I had chart paper. I reminded her that I'd put hers back. She said she knew that, but needed more. I was on my way out of the door, but told her where the pad was stored.

The day after my meeting with the principal and the middle school teacher, I went back to the vice principal's office a few minutes prior to my class to borrow the pad back. She was on the phone. Not wanting to be late, I went to my class, and sent a student to retrieve the chart paper. The student returned, saying that Miss Vee said she had used it all, but would get me some more.

Without the chart paper, I had to improvise a new plan for the challenging middle school class. The teacher who had been out, after his mother's passing, had returned. He brought the students to class, stating that he'd be happy to role play with me, since the upset students had refused to participate in the previous session. I had decided not to continue the roleplay, and to list their potential rules on chart paper instead, as the principal had suggested they have input into the rules, but without the paper, I decided to have a class discussion as an alternative.

I used my play-microphone to ask students to respond to two questions.

1: If you were in charge of your own country,
   what would one of the rules be?
2: If you were me, and in charge, of this class,
   what would one of the rules be?

I gave them the option to pass, and most of them did, and those who didn't came up with mostly silly rules, like, "everyone would read comics," or, "we could do whatever we want."

At some point, the vice principal also came to sit in on the class, and reprimanded a few unruly students for their disrespectful behavior. At the end of my improvised class, I invited the students to don costumes for my traditional class picture, but less than a third were interested. I was dismayed.

The next day, I got yet another email from the principal asking me to meet with her at the end of the week. The morning of our scheduled meeting she sent another email stating that she'd stayed home with a migraine, but asking me to meet with the vice-principal instead.

That day I'd learned, from a different middle school class, that some of the upper school students were in trouble for discarding, and replacing, items from the packed lunches of some of their peers.

When meeting with the vice-principal that second Friday of the school year, she'd said, "They need consequences."

"Ya think?" I thought to myself.

She went on to tell me that they had decided to go in "a different direction for the middle school," and that they wanted to dismantle my program.

I agreed that this was fine, given my experience so far, but relayed that when I'd provided my rates, my stated fee was thirty-five dollars an hour for anything less than twenty hours a week.

"However, since I'm already here, I can do it for thirty dollars an hour," I attempted to compromise.

My vice-principal promised to share my negotiated rate with my principal and get back to me.

The new scale would mean I'd lose twenty dollars a week, but gain four hours of free-time, so I considered it a good deal, particularly given that I'd recently obtained a new part-time position bartending at a local theater. I'd taken the second job to pay for my daughter's new expensive hobby of practicing cello, but knew that one additional shift a week would compensate for the lost income at my school. I also understood that being relieved of my most challenging age group would be well worth it.

The following Monday I received an email from the principal agreeing to the negotiated rate, and asking me to add her to the weekly lesson plan emails I was currently assigned to send to the vice-principal and third administrator. Great! No problem.

I ensured that my lesson plans were timely and detailed, and went about teaching my newly negotiated sixteen hours a week. For the next month or so, all was well. However, when I received my first reprieve from working (that election weekend), which should have given me four days off, as it also included a Monday of professional development for teachers that I was not required to attend, I received yet another email from the principal inquiring about a potential performance prior to our winter break. This made it difficult for me to enjoy the break, as I was now focused on how to respond to her request.

I replied, stating that a showcase was possible, and that I had been considering the possibility of a cabaret, after getting some advice from another colleague at the theater where I was bartending.

The principal replied, asking what a cabaret might look like, asking which of my classes were ready, and adding that she wanted the winter performance to be "inclusive."

I don't like getting too much into detail in emails, as I believe a lot gets lost in translation with tone and intention, so I asked for a meeting to discuss any further considerations in person. I was only allowed one planning period a week — an hour in between classes on Wednesdays — so I proposed this time for our meet-up.

The principal relayed that she wasn't available that week, but suggested that I meet with the vice-principal and third administrator. I agreed, but was told by the third administrator, let's call her Laura, that she and the vice-principal, Miss Vee, were responsible for half-day dismissal at that time. It took a few more days of back and forth emails to find a time that the other two administrators and I had mutual availability. We finally settled on a time at the end of the week after I first requested a face-to-face.

Upon said meeting, Laura and Miss Vee relayed that the lower school classes were creating their own winter programs, which I should offer to assist with; then asked if I would be willing to create a program for the four upper schools classes I still had. These were fourth to sixth-grade classes. I agreed.

I began working on the program immediately, but by then, there was only a week before our Thanksgiving break. The weekend of that break I received another email from the principal, stating that she was "concerned" that I had not coordinated dates for the programs, as this was "agreed upon in our contract."

I sent a response to an older email from the principal, where she'd asked if "we could start working to set dates," suggesting that I believed the "we" implied that we'd be working together, and that none of my previous contracts had required me to set dates by myself, as there was usually someone assigned, on behalf of the school, who was familiar with the calendar, to coordinate with. In this case, I thought it would be her, I relayed.

I did not receive a response to that email, but still sent another one to all of my administrators, just before the end of the holiday break, with potential suggestions for the upper school classes I had been assigned. One of the administrators responded that she was "worried" about one of my choices, "The Goofy Reindeer." They didn't want anything related to a religious holiday, unless, as in the case of the "Children's House" program, we included most, or all religions. I started to get frustrated then, as I had already been granted permission to do a "Kwanzaa Rap." Someone later explained that Kwanzaa was cultural, as opposed to religious, however. In a previous school showcase, I'd included Kwanzaa, Hanukkah, a play about "Holidays around the World" and "The Goofy Reindeer," a Christmas play. Given the fact that I'd been told the school would be split into three separate performances, this plan wouldn't work. I would need to change course.

At the end of the holiday weekend, I found a "winter poem" I could split between two classes, and copied it in an email to my administration. In addition to the Kwanzaa rap that one of the four classes had been assigned, I thought I could use the *Holidays around the World* multicultural play that my best class could pull off with minimal rehearsal.

Since I'd been informed that there was not enough room in the small auditorium for any of the three groups to perform together, I'd also been tasked with setting three different dates and times for the performances. After a week of back and forth between the teachers, we settled on dates for each.

After rehearsing with each class, along with my after school "Kids' Club," who had decided, after much adieu, to create a *Nutcracker* dance, I began to feel confident about our show.

Adding to my newfound conviction was a reading I'd discovered in a text gifted to me by the school. The passage I typed from Conscious Discipline: Building Resilient Classrooms, late one night, and assigned to various students in one class, was about universal energy and messages in various religions and cultures.

I felt this discovery a Godsend, and I sent it to my administrators the next day.

However, just two days after sharing this selection, I hit a wall. In my last class that Thursday, we were going through our breathe-in routine when the girl next to me started whispering to her neighbor. I tapped my hand against her upper thigh, saying, "Be quiet!"

I realized that my "tap" may have been more like a smack, as I heard it make a sound. I experienced a brief moment of panic. "What if she thinks I hit her?" I thought to myself.

However, realizing I couldn't have possibly hurt her, as the tap was just on the meat of her thigh, I brushed off the thought, and continued the class. One of the one-on-one teachers, who was substituting for the usual one-on-one was a bit overzealous, and was taking over my "emotion charades" activity, but I decided to let him, as I issued another student who was mis-behaving for a third time a behavior journal for interrupting and touching other students. I sent him to our "book nook" in the hallway to complete his journal, and returned to our game. Another adult, who was a permanent one-on-one assistant, and always very supportive and helpful approached me.

"Did you hit Shayla?" she asked.

"No," I replied. I explained, and then demonstrated to her what had occurred.

"I didn't think so," the assistant said, "but she told me you hit her. You might want to talk to her so she doesn't go home and say that."

Just then, another teaching assistant poked his head in from the hallway and asked what my student, who was in the hallway, was supposed to be doing.

I had honestly forgotten about sending him out, so at first I thought he'd left on his own. When I saw him with the clipboard I remembered that I'd given him the behavior journal and walked him through the questions, and the process for completing it. I was able to help him in the hallway since the substitute one-on-one had already taken over the lesson.

When I returned, we wrapped up our game of charades, as the class was coming to an end. As the students lined up to leave, I asked for a few student volunteers to help us set up the tables for the chess club that used my room on Thursdays. I thought about talking to Shayla, but when she volunteered to stay after, I let her, thinking that her willingness to help out probably meant she'd let the incident go.

I let it go too, and went through the next day's classes, preparing for the winter showcase as usual. Five minutes before the end of my last class that afternoon, another teaching assistant showed up, stating that she'd been asked to cover my class so that I could meet with the vice-principal.

This was the assistant I had been friendly with, in the beginning of the year, before I'd been informed that she'd relayed to the principal that she was disappointed in my handling of the middle school class before the program was dismantled.

"Did anything happen?" she asked, as I gathered my water bottle and keys, after instructing my last class in what to do with their final five minutes.

I thought, briefly, about the former day's incident, but dismissed the thought, stating instead, "I sent her an email a couple of days ago about the winter program. Maybe she wants to discuss that."

When I arrived at the office, however, I saw Shayla sitting at a table, looking smug, and I quickly realized what this meeting would be about. My heart began to race. The vice-principal invited me into the principal's office, and shared that Shayla had, indeed, gone home to say that I hit her.

"Her father called, and he was livid," she stated. She used that word "livid" a couple of times, before I found myself feeling livid as well.

The vice principal explained that Shayla said, "You popped her like her mama pops her." I tried to explain what took place.

"You can't," she said.

"I know," I replied.

She reiterated that Shayla's father was "livid."

"This is why she acts the way she acts," I said, thinking of all that I sacrificed for my students, and that this man, who'd never met me would believe I'd ever hurt a child.

"You know..." I began, then interrupted myself, "No, you don't know me."

I fought the tears that began welling up at the implication that I was in the wrong here.

"*She said, 'you popped her like her mama pops her.*'" Yes, I thought to myself, it was a "church mama pop" on the leg, something most any mama would do to correct her child, but I didn't, physically, *hurt* her. I would never! I felt that the fact that I always treat these children like my own was being used against me. I don't beat my own child, but sure, I'd "tap" her thigh if she were out of line.

Most days, I'd simply call the parent, in such an instance, and let them discipline their own child at home. She was right. I knew I wasn't allowed to touch them, especially in any sort of punitive way. Of course, I gave hugs and held hands, but any physical reprimand was out of order, and I knew better.

I wish I could adequately explain to you, reader, how many times I've "popped" my own thigh, in an attempt to understand what happened that afternoon. Even when I do so, even much harder than I can possibly imagine having done it to her, I am inclined to believe that the only pain I inflicted was to her ego.

After much conversation, with friends and family about the incident, I must acknowledge, humbly, however, that her pain threshold may have been different than mine. Is it probable that I physically hurt her? No. Is it possible though? It is, and that haunts me.

None of these were perfect moments, and I am only human. So, if you must judge me, then, at least honor the teachers who haven't resorted to such measures; and, at best, understand the kind of stress I've detailed here that lead to such lapses in my own good judgment. If you are feeling uneasy, rest assured that I would never repeat the behavior. If I had it to do again, I would have whispered the admonishment, with no physical accompaniment of any sort. If I'd been more tempered, I would have done exactly that. Maybe that's part of my point though. Quite honestly, I don't ever want to be put in a position where I have twenty-six students in a class again. I plan to never subject myself to the kind of stress that would lead me to this level of irritation. I only share this incident, now, on behalf of the many other teachers who lost employment due to similar circumstances, and trust me, there has been plenty of debate, as to whether I should share it at all.

"Well, I guess I'll need you to write a statement," the vice-principal said, handing me a piece of paper and a pen, and joking about the silly pen she gave me.

I wrote a quick statement, detailing the events of the previous day, stating that I understood how my "tap" could have been misconstrued as a "pop," and promising to keep my hands to myself, henceforth.

It had been a long week, and I was looking forward to getting home, and having enough wine to numb the pain of working so hard for so little, and being underappreciated, and then accused of hurting a child! I left my statement on the vice principal's desk, and returned to my room to collect my belongings.

I stopped a few doors down to chat with the assistant who'd been in my room the day of the incident, and the one who had taken over my class. I explained the situation, and they were both incredulous.

"I understand," said the one who had taken over my class, "we don't even get paid enough to deal with all of this."

"My last check was seven-hundred dollars, for two weeks," I sighed.

The assistant who was in the room proffered, "if you'd really hit her, the students would have said something. You know they catch everything."

"Exactly," I cosigned, then headed down the hall.

On the way, I encountered a teacher who apologized for sending her very challenging class late, the day before. I told her I understood her obstacles.

"Is my class that much worse than everyone else's?" she asked. They were, but I joked, "As I told Mr. K (who had the worst lower school class; she had the worst upper school class), the fact that you have them means you're either really good, or they don't like you."

"Maybe it's both," she half-joked back.

I went back to my room to grab my purse and lock up. I was on the way out of the door, when I decided to stop back in the office to sign out and ensure the vice principal had received my statement.

When I entered the office, one of the administrative assistants informed me that the vice-principal and principal wanted to speak with me.

I went back into the principal's office and took a few deep breaths as I waited for them to arrive. What was taking so long?! I really just wanted to go home.

They entered together, with the principal standing behind me, and the vice-principal in front of me. The V.P. said, "I haven't had a chance to speak with Ms. N (the assistant who'd been in the room) or any of the other students, but Shayla says you hit her, and her friend says you hit her, and you said 'this is why she acts the way she acts.' We *have* to let you go."

I didn't have the energy to argue with her. I'd felt, for a while, that I wasn't valued there, and I try not to stay anywhere my gifts aren't appreciated, so I simply responded, "Okay. Y'all have a good weekend. I'll be back next week to get my things." I saw Ms. N outside, as I was leaving, and told her, "They let me go."

She gasped in disbelief. I said my goodbyes to her, and a few of the students, without making a big scene, and headed home.

I took a long weekend to process, told my mom, daughter and a few close friends what had transpired, and went back on Tuesday, with my child, to collect my materials.

My daughter asked if it would be awkward. I admitted that it might be. I was glad I chose to sign in at the office, rather than attempting to swipe my entry card at the back door, because when I tried to swipe it to gain re-entry during the moving process, I found it had already been deactivated.

I'd come after school, so as to gain access to the limited parking available in the back lot, so I didn't get to see many of my students, but I left my door open as we packed, and explained the reason for my departure to a couple of inquisitive upper elementary students in the after school program who happened to pass by.

When my daughter and I had finished removing my fabrics, and student pictures from the walls, and I had packed up some seven boxes and four crates of materials, I returned to the office to leave my key and copy card. I ran into one of the teachers on one of our car runs, and she'd relayed that she was taking over the winter production. I promised to leave all of the materials in her box, and was able to retrieve them from recycling shortly thereafter. In addition to leaving copies of scripts, poems, songs and setlists, my daughter helped put a copy of each of the costumed class pictures, labeled with names into each teacher's box. I saw a few more students on my way out, and gave hugs. Some asked me what happened, and the students I'd spoken with earlier began reciting the information they'd been given. I told the others I couldn't speak about it then, but that I would.

At the time of this writing, it had been six weeks since my firing, and I'd been underemployed ever since. Fortunately, I'd taken on that second-part time job bartending at our local theater in exchange for minimum wage, tips and free theater tickets, in order to fund my daughter's sudden interest in cello lessons. That gig, and a Christmas gift from my sister, paid my January bills, but I had yet to find alternate employment, as my mind was set on not returning to teaching. I was tired of being disrespected for a living.

I wasn't sure what the future held, but now that this chapter, and this book was complete, I looked forward to finally accomplishing my mission of sharing the teacher's side of the story when it comes to our educational crisis in America. I pray that some will be inspired by my story, and use it to affect change, whether it be through policy, teaching, administration or parenting. As always, I am sincerely grateful to you, dear reader, for taking the time to read these words. Upward and Onward.

-Asia Maxton
 Retired Superwoman
 January 21, 2019

WHAT'S MY POINT?

It had been a very long time since I'd added to this story. I wrote myself a few notes, in the meantime. When I taught language arts, there were three guiding questions I'd always ask my students.

1. What's my point?
2. Who cares?
3. Why?

As I began to wrap up this writing, I continued to ask myself:

1. What I want you, the reader, to take away from your reading?
2. Who are you, dear reader?
3. Why should you care about my story?
4. What do I want you to *do* once you've read it?

I can begin by telling you that I came up with my original title after watching the 2010 film, "Waiting for Superman." My take-away from that documentary was that teachers were getting a bad rep for a systemic problem. I wanted you, the reader, to understand just what we teachers were up against, and how even a great teacher could become bitter, quickly, within such a set-up. So, the working title for this book was I'm Not Your Superwoman. I wanted my readers to know that we teachers

are human, and though we often pride ourselves on our "superpowers" or gifts, we are not, in fact, superhuman, and it is unfair to expect us to be.

I changed the title both because I love alliteration, and because I thought it would give you all a better idea of what you can actually expect from this reading.

As I've written, I also came to the realization that this book may also be for teachers entering the system, at risk of becoming disenchanted, to catch glimpses of what worked in my career.

One note I made sure to include, for all of you, is how much I understand now that our students, desperately, want to be involved in their learning, and their lives.

As the old Benjamin Franklin quote reads, "Tell me and I forget, teach me and I may remember, involve me and I learn."

That said, some of the ways I've been able to involve my students in their learning is through offering class jobs. When I was teaching full-time, I'd ask my students to write resumes and cover letters for these jobs, so they'd take them seriously. Since switching back to part-time, I often change these duties based upon class performance. My students get to choose our warmup game, by lottery, but only if they've been entered because they were focused during our class breathe-in. I often let them use their fingers to choose between choices of activities. For example, "put up a 'one' if you'd like me to rap the rules a cappella, and a 'two' if you'd like me to rap with a beat."

I've asked students to participate in developing a performance rubric, then allowed them to choose whether to let their peers judge them on each criterion, by scoring them with the same finger system. I was pleasantly surprised by how much they enjoyed giving, and receiving, feedback this way.

In summer camp, our older students have loved being stage crew, participating as runners, assistants, lights, costume and prop masters while our younger students perform.

Students have begged me to do simple tasks like turn out the lights before our breathe-in, or choose the music for our reflection, reminding me that they simply want to be involved in any, and all, aspects of their learning. As I think about the adults I know, self included, this no longer surprises me. Most of us, simply, want as much agency over our lives as we can handle. Why should our children be any different?

P.S. At the time of my second revision, March 9, 2019, I had accepted another part-time teaching position. This time, however, I was only teaching two classes a week, and was compensated for 3.5 hours a day at 35 dollars an hour, despite only teaching those two one-hour classes. I had the same thirteen students both days, and had recently been gifted with a teaching assistant. Ironically, I was teaching these classes at the school where I first taught full-time through my residency program. A local arts agency sponsored this after-school program. I managed to stay afloat financially, picking up a few extra bartending shifts, and still paid rent with my tax refund that year.

As of the third revision, June 23rd, 2020, I was teaching three classes a week in that after school program before the Coronavirus closed schools. I was also, finally able, that year, to accept an adjunct faculty position at Coppin State University, teaching speech and acting classes. I taught 3 classes per semester for them that school year as well. This means, before the pandemic, I was making twice as much teaching twelve total classes a week, as I'd made the prior two years teaching nineteen to twenty classes a week. My class sizes in both my after school and college classes are also, almost half the size of what I'd been teaching as well. My largest class size this year was 18 students in a college-level speech class. My average class size was 15 students. The impact this reduction had on my teaching, and my sanity, is immeasurable.

I am happier than I have been in a very long time, and I would recommend that anyone who is as stressed as I was reexamine their worth, and have faith in themselves, and the process.

Thank you for reading.

WHO CARES?

As I prepared to wrap up this writing, a co-worker said, "I think most people know that teachers have it hard. I'm not sure we know what we can do about it."

I found this to be an excellent point, so I shall conclude with a list of action steps that those of you who took the time to read this far can take:

- Volunteer to mentor one child. At the time of my second draft of this memoir, I was eagerly awaiting a position I'd applied for, as what I'd started to refer to as a "Mentor Matchmaker." My time in education has shown me that our youth are desperate for individual attention. The name of the program I applied for is C.H.I.P. (Children Having Incarcerated Parents), but I have also served as a mentor through Big Brothers/ Big Sisters, once in an informal capacity through my spiritual center and, another time, through a chance encounter during my time in the school system. While I did not get the position with C.H.I.P., I still encourage one-on-one mentorship as a solution to the challenges we face.

- Parent! It is one of the most challenging things to do well, and I've been still struggling with my, now, sixteen year-old, but it is critical. Read with your children. Talk to your children. Find out their passions and locate the resources that will support them! There are plenty of in-school, after school, and summer school opportunities for developing your student's skill sets; many of them are free. Seek to be active partners with their teachers. Take your responsibility seriously, and encourage your friends and family to do the same.

• Volunteer in the schools. Choose a local, or high-needs, school and offer your services. You can be a reading partner, fundraiser, or even assist with "small" tasks like copying. It generally just requires a background check and a meeting with a teacher or principal to assess the need, and "get in where you fit in."

• Donate. I often say that when I don't have the money, I have the time, but when I have the money, I don't have the time. If you have a little extra money, but not time — find a school or organization you are willing to support, and put your money where your heart is. Also, support the fundraising efforts in place at your local public institutions.

• Get informed and VOTE. Not just in presidential elections, but in local elections. Hold our politicians accountable for serving our students. If you don't feel informed enough, you are not alone. Get comfortable speaking to people you respect and trust about politics. Ask questions, and show up for every vote. Politicians take note of who is voting, and what their interests are, even if they are pandering to us. Make them pander and respond to our values, and our children's needs.

• Get involved! Attend school board meetings, PTA meetings and School and Family Council Meetings. Listen, and offer what you can to assist.

• Support your favorite teachers! Often a note of acknowledgement, an email, small gift or word of encouragement keeps us going in this ultra-challenging field.

At the time of this fifth, and final, revision, August 11, 2020, many of our schools have been closed due to the worldwide pandemic known as Covid-19, or the Coronavirus. Many of us have gone virtual as a result of this crisis. Now, more than ever, we have the opportunity to reimagine education, and to collaborate with each other to do so. In the past month, I have offered a virtual workshop on theatre, and taken another. I attended another free workshop on *The Somatic Integration on Emotional Intelligence,* and plan to offer a few workshops of my own in the near future. It has been my dream to teach teachers for a while now. I learned so much through trial and error, and I want to share my knowledge and experience with educators in order to benefit our children, and our world. Please reach out if you would be interested in a workshop for your organization. While I can no longer operate in the system as it stands, education remains my passion.

WHY?

"I have come to believe that a great teacher is a great artist and that there are as few as there are any other great artists. Teaching might even be the greatest of the arts since the medium is the human mind and spirit."
- John Steinbeck

There is a poem that I've written, that I now begin my theatre classes with. I call it an "I am" poem, one written in grad school, that has also become my mission statement.

Here it is:

Trying to find something productive to do is harder than I'd imagined
No numbers to call, or pictures to draw
Driving myself up a wall
Hard to climb
When my mind is on all the wrong things
I can't sing or dance
No time for romance
Many minutes 'til midnight
I can't quite sit still
Allow my mind to roam
Thoughts and plots
Of how to kill — myself
Might manifest in my mental

It's simple really
But no time to be silly
Or cry
Shows to perform, books to write
Wanna upgrade my standard of living
God-willing
Take a deep breath
Get some stuff of my chest
And live life 'til my death
Gotta get correct
Keep myself in check
Bounce back —
And take another giant step
Reach for the moon
Or settle 'mongst the stars
Listen to my homegirls
Play acoustic guitars
Eight more bars
in the cell in which I dwell
Thanksgiving 'cuz I'm living
I have stories to tell
Use my body as a vessel
And my mind as an oar
Send out a beam of light
Help someone else find the shore
Can't wallow in the shallow end too long
Born black and a woman, born strong
When the ride gets rough
I'll hold on
Not too far gone,
But gone too far

To hold back any longer
I was born to be a star
Fish float, slackers coast
Stay humble, don't boast
But at my funeral
I want to make my own toast
She laughed, she lived
She had a kid
She spread peace, love and joy
She's done 'cuz she did
She met hatred with humanity
She wrote, she writ
She suffered, she struggled
But she just wouldn't quit
She inspired, she shared
She made use of her gifts
God is good
Though life's not fair
She's gone back home
We'll see her there

Many of the questions regarding why I spent four years dedicated to this project are answered by the poem. I want to inspire and share by telling my stories and using my gifts.

At the time of this writing, Covid-19 has ravaged our nation, and made its rounds through the world. We have learned, in this time, that America struggled to contain the pandemic, while many similar nations have already recovered. It is my belief that our country's focus on individualism is partially to blame for this failure, while our overall lack of education is also at fault. In order to survive, let alone thrive, we must find a collective way to encourage a consciousness of caring for each other. Furthermore, we need to learn to read, study and apply information, particularly science, math and critical thought. In order to do this, we have to find a way to enroll, and retain, our brightest minds in the field of education. This will be an impossible task as long as teachers are undervalued, and thrust into a system of indentured servitude that disallows those who have burned out, or were lackluster to begin with, to find alternate means of employment. In countries like Finland, that have the best education systems, educators are thoroughly trained, and given the freedom to teach, as they have already proven themselves to be the cream of the crop.

In the field of education, we are encouraged to use essential questions to guide our lessons and units of learning, so I'll elaborate on the question of "why?" by asking some questions of the reader here.

How might we encourage our best and brightest to not only enter, but persist in, the field of education?

How might we support our students, particularly our most challenged, in valuing their education?

How might we assist families and communities in investing in their children's education?

How might we reimagine education in a way that engages, and best serves, the disenfranchised?

In closing, here are a few thoughts from my fellow Teachers:

"Remember the importance of children's Social-Emotional Development. It is important that kids understand that they have feelings and thoughts on life, love, school, family and other issues and that those thoughts and feelings are important, relevant and right! Those feelings and emotions should be heard and discussed so that children know that they aren't alone and that it's healthy to have and express feelings. Provide kids with an outlet, journal, therapist, or simply a non-judgmental ear to listen."
- Rell Lucas, Elementary, middle school teacher

"Focus on the whole child. Schools provide food, clothing, and healthy activities to the community. Find ways to partner with community organizations to support schools. Use your time and talents to give back."
- Keyonna Saunders, 4th grade teacher

"Focus on relationships. Instill confidence in your students by celebrating them and letting them know that you genuinely care."
- Kevin Older, 6th-8th grade math teacher

"Connect students with opportunities outside of school. I'm pretty well connected in the writing world. When students tell me they want to become writers, I talk with them about getting published and expose them to opportunities to do so. Schools are too insular, with too

little emphasis on the school and not the world we're preparing them for."
- B. Sharise Moore, 6th grade Language Arts teacher

"From the research I did on teacher demoralization in the U.S., I would recommend folks supporting and joining teacher movements that are demanding more resources in schools such as counselors, nurses, social workers, less standardized testing, and culturally competent curricula."
- Odessa Armstrong, former colleague and middle school Language Arts teacher

RESOURCES

BOOKS

Classroom Management for Art, Music, and PE Teachers
Michale Linsin

Think and Grow Rich: A Black Choice
Dennis Kimbro, Napoleon Hill

Teach Like a Champion:
49 Techniques that Put Students on the Path to College
Doug Lemov

Conscious Discipline: Building Resilient Classrooms
Dr. Becky A. Bailey

"Ordinary" Children, Extraordinary Teachers
Marva Collins

The Law of Attraction:
The Basics of the Teachings of Abraham
Esther and Jerry Hicks

An Ethic of Excellence:
Building a Culture of Craftsmanship with Students
Ron Berger

Desmond and the Very Mean Word
Desmond Tutu and Douglas Carlton Abrams

R.A.C.E. RAP
RESTATE. ANSWER. CITE. EXTEND.
(FOR TEACHING WRITING)

Teacher reads first lines, students respond with bolded second lines

Restate the question
that is the lesson

Answer ALL of the question
don't you just guess, then

Cite some examples
straight from the text

now extend your response
Yeah, you know what comes next

Relate it to you
Tell them why this is true

Your conclusion sentence was so very cool
Now 1, 2, 3, 4

Show those 5th graders their score
A 3 for me, Oh yeah, I've got it

So well that I could have taught it

BIG CLASS GOALS

The following is a "note" I wrote on Facebook about the BIG class goals:

1) Develop a love of learning. Curiosity is the gift that has led to GREAT discovery. Read. Write. Share. Investigate. Channel your inner four-year old and ask "Why?"

2) Reading and Writing Fluency — This is, the ability to digest and disseminate information accurately and rapidly. Come on! This is the 21st century. All of the knowledge that we need to know, and to share, is available at our fingertips.

3) Support Each Other. No one I know, who is truly great has gone it alone. We are "not in this by ourselves" because we need each other. To get, you must give! There is a song we sing at my spiritual center which goes "We are all angels…who only have one wing…all angels…searching for each other…We are all angels…who cannot reach the sky…'cause we need each other…to fly!" Amen!

4) Know your strengths and weaknesses. One of my students asked me this year how I come up with ideas and write them out so rapidly. I told him "this is my gift." However, if you buy some furniture and give me a diagram to put it together Well…he replied, "That is my gift."

5) Know when to ask for help. Another student was trying to post a sign that was too high for her to reach. When I reminded her of this goal, she responded "Yes, but I should try first, right?" Touché!

6) Use Your Resources. Whether this means Google, Research, Library, Computers, Friends. Start where you are with what you have…and prepare to be amazed.

7) Think critically:
   The 3 essential questions that underlie my class are:
   1) What's my point?
   2) Who cares?
   3) Why?

   This means that you should think about your intended audience, make them care! And find out what matters to them when speaking or writing.

   When reading ask:
   What is their point?
   Why do I care?
   How did they make me care?
   What did they do to/how did they…make me care?

SCHOOL PLAYLISTS

PLAYLIST ONE*

The following is a selection from the playlist link available below.

RISE UP

ANDRA DAY

SUPERSTAR

LUPE FIASCO, MATTHEW SANTOS

CONQUEROR

ESTELLE

FIXER UPPER

FROM "FROZEN"; MAIA WILSON, "FROZEN" CAST

LIGHTS

DAMIEN ESCOBAR

THIS IS ME

KEALA SETTLE FROM "THE GREATEST SHOWMAN"

CINEMATIC

OWL CITY

*https://tidal.com/playlist/ccd5dc18-5186-4acb-b9f7-77802ad01201

EVERYBODY
RAUL MIDÓN

I BELIEVE
DJ KHALED, DEMI LAVATO

WHAT IF
INDIA.ARIE

STAND UP FOR SOMETHING
ANDRA DAY, COMMON

JUST DO YOU
INDIA.ARIE

BALTIMORE
NINA SIMONE

FREEDOM
PHARRELL WILLIAMS

GOLDEN
JILL SCOTT

PLAYLIST TWO*

WAKE UP EVERYBODY
JOHN LEGEND, THE ROOTS, COMMON AND MELANIE FIONA

WHEN I WAKE UP
JILL SCOTT

WAKE UP
ALICIA KEYS

LOVELY DAY
BILL WITHERS

GOTTA GET UP (ANOTHER DAY) MINNIE VERSION
JILL SCOTT

BRAND NEW ME
ALICIA KEYS

NO
MEGHAN TRAINOR

RUN THE WORLD (GIRLS)
BEYONCÉ

THE STRONG SURVIVE
NIKKI LYNETTE

*https://open.spotify.com/playlist/01VoJDkmjLs7qNMO0MFlyr

IFU
VENUS 7

DREAM SONG
VENUS 7

STATE OF MIND
RAUL MIDÓN

I CAN
NAS

BE GREAT
EZE JACKSON

THE GREATEST SHOW
HUGH JACKMAN, KEALA SETTLE, ZAC EFRON, ZENDAYA,
THE GREATEST SHOWMAN ENSEMBLE

SHINE
JOHN LEGEND, THE ROOTS

BRAVE
SARA BAREILLES

BEAUTIFUL
CHRISTINA AGUILERA

BABY I'M A STAR
PRINCE

PHOENIX
DAMIEN ESCOBAR

BALTIMORE
JAZMINE SULLIVAN

WE ARE YOUNG, GIFTED AND BLACK
COMMON, LALAH HATHAWAY

SCARS TO YOUR BEAUTIFUL
ALESSIA CARA

WHERE IS THE LOVE?
BLACK EYED PEAS

THERE'S HOPE
INDIA.ARIE

JUST DO YOU
INDIA.ARIE

SUPERWOMAN
ALICIA KEYS

ONLINE RESOURCES

GREAT MEDITATION/BREATHE-IN MUSIC ALBUM ASIAN ZEN: MEDITATION

https://listen.tidal.com/album/38928162/track/38928163

Suggested Breathing Technique:

Inhale for 6 seconds

Hold for 7 seconds

Exhale for 8 seconds

FREE COMMUNITY-BUILDING EXERCISES FROM REDBARN:

youtube.com/channel/UCte7x_6Rvhk-ed-0k0qCMuQ

WORKSHOP:

sarayanneydance.com/somatic-integration-of-emotional-intelligence-2/

OBJECTIVE AND TACTICS EXERCISE

OBJECTIVE
What do you want? List one short or long-term goal.

TACTICS
How will you get it?
List at least 2 strategies for obtaining your objective.

OBSTACLES
What might get in your way?
List at least 2 obstacles to fulfilling your goal.

MOTIVATION
Why do you want what you want?
Make sure that your motivation is strong enough to overcome
your obstacles.

For workshops, contact: missazya@gmail.com

ACKNOWLEDGEMENTS

Thank you, first and foremost, to all of the students I have had the pleasure to serve. I hope I've honored you in your reflections and representations. Please reach out with your feedback. To my colleagues and peers, thank you for teaching me, working with me and tolerating me through the years. Azania, dearest daughter, thank you for sharing not only me, with the world, but so many of your own books, toys and supplies over the years. I owe you, and I've got you! Thank you sister, Ashindi, for sponsoring the book cover, and for supporting me over the years with unconditional love. Mommy, Sally Maxton, I've said it here, and I'll say it again, one day I will manage to pay you back for having my back all of this time. You are the prototype. Thank you! Daddy, Reginald Maxton, you've been tied with mom for my number two fan all of these years. I wish, for every child, a cheerleader like you! One day, I may make a play out of your voicemails alone. Ingrid Sibley, you brilliant, brutal and beautiful editor — you are my Day One and will be my Day 10 Million. I love you forever! Nikki, thank you for nightly chats and insight. You, and writing, are my therapists. I am honored to be one of your counselors as well. Twelve, always twelve! Facebook family, you read all of my original posts, and your reactions and comments kept me going. Thank you! Shout out to all of my teachers! You paved the way, and I am grateful. To those of you who've read this far: I am forever honored by your willingness to receive my words in this way. Thank you! Thanks to Young Audiences/Arts for Learning, the Baltimore City Teaching Residency, John Ruhrah, Brehms Lane,

City Neighbors Hamilton, Bring the Noise, Leaders of Tomorrow Youth Center, Baltimore Montessori, Creative Alliance, Everyman Theatre, Center Stage and Coppin State University for all of the lessons and learning. Thank you Deletta Gillespie for putting me on to Coppin. Dr. Ra Sheem Shvilla and Ti Coleman, thank you for helping me to believe in myself again, and for all of your support and scholarship. Dr. Garey Hyatt, thank you for your guidance. I forgot some people. We always do — but your spirit matters, and I am grateful.

Please insert your name here: